The *Heart*

of *God*

Robert Benjamin Bamburg

The Heart of God

ISBN-13: 978-0615765297 (Paperback)
ISBN-10: 0615765297

To my Dad,

who showed me the heart of a father,
being my protector, provider, and counselor.

CONTENTS

WHAT IS GOD'S HEART?

Honestly, what is God's heart? To be known. We often have a perverted desire to be known. We'd like to become famous, have everyone know our name, and value our opinion just because. Who do we "know"? Actors, musicians, writers, entertainers... Do we even know our friends, our family... ourselves? What we seek to know, we don't even care. The reason we read about gossip is because someone has entertained us with fiction, with a story, and not even a true one, and if it is based on a true story we don't follow the character, but the actor. We seek a facade. We try to put on a facade. I was one of the shyest kids growing up, but for some odd reason I could play on the praise and worship team, I could act in the drama team, but if it came time for me to speak, I would tremble. Why? When you act, you do not make yourself vulnerable. No one can disagree with an act. No one can disagree with music. If one speaks from the heart, then you can make enemies very quickly. Sharing those thoughts and ideas can trigger hatred.

Enter Jesus. Here comes the Truth amidst all these actors, these self-righteous teachers of the law. He exposes them, and the crowd goes wild, they love hearing about their bad rap like we love celebrity gossip. Then Jesus turns to the crowd and exposes them. Many of them stop cheering, they join the teachers, they mock Jesus in defense. Jesus comes with humility willing to serve everyone, yet when he reveals who he truly is, the Son of God, the people hate him for it. They don't want to know him. They want to be served by him, or kill him.

We do the same thing. We say we want Jesus, "but do not expose my sins, don't seek to know me and my weaknesses. I don't need a savior, I want a servant and a shallow friend. Heal me, provide for me, give an ear, but don't ask anything of me."

What we don't realize is, He is love, not judgment. We fear the judgment. We don't want to let go of our hearts' desires, we don't want to admit faults, we are afraid of becoming slaves. "God don't send me to Africa, don't take my wealth from me, I don't want to yield, because I don't know you, and I don't want to know you. You are a hard man, you take from us what we tried so hard to create, you expect more from us than what we can offer, you created hell, you've killed, you've destroyed, even a good man you found no fault in you allowed to be tortured, your servants are murdered. What good could possibly come from you? Yet... you created me and the world, and I have some provisions, I... I'll try to please you and do a few good deeds, be a good person anyway and hope maybe you will have mercy on me and I might be able to avoid the judgment and punishment of hell."

I had a relationship somewhat like that with my father. I loved him, but I didn't know him well. We didn't relate to each other. I wasn't interested in going to Home Depot with him, or working on projects. He wasn't interested in video games, but we compromised from time to time. He would often work late, get stressed on the job, bring the tension home and sometimes lose his cool with us. I thought he was a "hard man". I appreciated having food on the table, but I couldn't understand why he acted that way. After I became an adult I realized I didn't see him home often because he wanted one parent with us all the time, and he paid for private school when we were kids to try to shelter us since we didn't live in a "nice" neighborhood. His job required him to think on a higher level with computers so trying to dumb himself down to a kid's level was extremely difficult. As a child, I could not reason his actions.

If only your eyes were opened to who God is and his heart. You could see that everything He does He does for a reason and out of love. His rules, even his "judgment" is out of love. The scary God of the Old Testament was scary because of his jealous love. God tried to protect his people from evil. There were lands who practiced the sacrificing of their babies, having sex with children, animals, things that go way beyond just stealing and cheating. He wiped them out for good reason. God is holy. Holy is a word that describes his type of perfect love; one that has no selfishness in it at all.

The fear of losing riches, yes there's a reason for that fear. God may cause them to slip through your fingers. However, in people going to Africa, those with AIDS and without parents may find love. Your loss of riches may result in you finding something greater.

"If anyone would come after me, he must deny himself and take up his cross and follow me. For whoever wants to save his life will lose it, but whoever loses his life for me will find it."
- Matthew 16:24-25 NIV

Notes:

How you have fallen from heaven, O morning star, son of the dawn! You have been cast down to the earth, you who once laid low the nations! 13 You said in your heart, "I will ascend to heaven; I will raise my throne above the stars of God; I will sit enthroned on the mount of assembly, on the utmost heights of the sacred mountain. 14 I will ascend above the tops of the clouds; I will make myself like the Most High." 15 But you are brought down to the grave, to the depths of the pit. - Isaiah 14:12-15 NIV

The word of the LORD came to me: 12 "Son of man, take up a lament concerning the king of Tyre and say to him: 'This is what the Sovereign LORD says: " 'You were the model of perfection, full of wisdom and perfect in beauty. 13 You were in Eden, the garden of God; every precious stone adorned you: ruby, topaz and emerald, chrysolite, onyx and jasper, sapphire, turquoise and beryl. Your settings and mountings were made of gold; on the day you were created they were prepared. 14 You were anointed as a guardian cherub, for so I ordained you. You were on the holy mount of God; you walked among the fiery stones. 15 You were blameless in your ways from the day you were created till wickedness was found in you. 16 Through your widespread trade you were filled with violence, and you sinned. So I drove you in disgrace from the mount of God, and I expelled you, O guardian cherub, from among the fiery stones. 17 Your heart became proud on account of your beauty, and you corrupted your wisdom because of your splendor. So I threw you to the earth; I made a spectacle of you before kings. - Ezekiel 28:11-17 NIV

Therefore rejoice, you heavens and you who dwell in them! But woe to the earth and the sea, because the devil has gone down to you! He is filled with fury, because he knows that his time is short." - Revelation 12:12 NIV

Information about Satan before the fall is typically written from a prophecy and a little ambiguous often referring to both the devil and a human being used as one of his instruments (i.e. King of Babylon, Tyre or the anti-christ) because he tempts men with the same desire he had and causes them to mimic him. Even Adam in Genesis 3:5 is told that he will be like God if he disobeys in eating the fruit.

CHAPTER 1

GOD'S PURPOSE

God's purpose has always been to share, just as a family desires to love and be loved. As a man loves a woman and wants to share an experience together, so He desires to love and be one with his creation. However, he gave his creation freewill and somehow, somewhere, it rejected him.

We know the story of creation: God creates the universe, then fine tunes the earth and fills it with life, and makes everything good in preparation for his greatest work. But before that happens there is discord in heaven with an angel named Lucifer. He desires to be higher and elevate himself. He desires to be greater than God, and God will not allow it. He casts Lucifer down along with the angels that joined with him totaling a third of heaven. This is important to note because...

God creates man in his very own image and appreciates him more than all creation. Lucifer, or Satan, as he has become known, sees this and burns with envy. Satan saw the opportunity to defame God in tempting Adam with the same thoughts he had. He told Adam he could become like God. The fallen wanted to replace God. God understood Adam was deceived and devised a way to prove to Satan that his will could not be undone nor hindered, as well as show his unfailing love towards man. He invited his creation to join Him in his work and all the while Satan tried to corrupt the image of God.

Notes:

Then the LORD said to Satan, "Have you considered my servant Job? There is no one on earth like him; he is blameless and upright, a man who fears God and shuns evil." 9 "Does Job fear God for nothing?" Satan replied. 10 "Have you not put a hedge around him and his household and everything he has? You have blessed the work of his hands, so that his flocks and herds are spread throughout the land. 11 But stretch out your hand and strike everything he has, and he will surely curse you to your face." - Job 1:8-11 NIV

At this, Job got up and tore his robe and shaved his head. Then he fell to the ground in worship 21 and said: "Naked I came from my mother's womb, and naked I will depart. The LORD gave and the LORD has taken away; may the name of the LORD be praised." 22 In all this, Job did not sin by charging God with wrongdoing. - Job 1:20-22 NIV

And God blessed them. And God said to them, "Be fruitful and multiply and fill the earth and subdue it and have dominion over the fish of the sea and over the birds of the heavens and over every living thing that moves on the earth." - Genesis 1:28 ESV

And God blessed Noah and his sons and said to them, "Be fruitful and multiply and fill the earth. - Genesis 9:1 ESV

and said, "By myself I have sworn, declares the LORD, because you have done this and have not withheld your son, your only son, 17 I will surely bless you, and I will surely multiply your offspring as the stars of heaven and as the sand that is on the seashore. And your offspring shall possess the gate of his enemies, 18 and in your offspring shall all the nations of the earth be blessed, because you have obeyed my voice." Genesis 22:16-18 ESV

Greater love has no one than this, that someone lay down his life for his friends. - John 15:13 ESV

God saw something special in Abraham, Job, David, and others.

Satan tried to tarnish Job causing terrible things to happen to him for no good reason. Through it all Job proved God's character to Satan and to his friends. Job never defamed God, but instead remained faithful and thus made Satan's plans futile.

Satan then turns the whole earth away hoping to destroy everyone who bears the image of God. However, he cannot turn Noah. God starts over with his family making the same covenant with him as Adam, "Be fruitful and multiply and spread throughout the earth." But his lineage also disobeys, stays in one place and builds a monument, the Tower of Babel, to themselves. God causes them to obey by confusing their languages and making them disperse. He calls a certain man out from Babylon/Chaldeans named Abram. This man loves God so much that he is willing to offer his own son, and God sees that there is no greater sacrifice, no greater love that a man could give. He makes a covenant with Abraham basically saying, "you are exactly what I was hoping for". Abraham giving up his promised son, reminds me of a Charlie and the Chocolate Factory moment with him giving up the everlasting gobstopper (giving away his assurance/hope of a promise), but anyway. God gives Abraham this inheritance and says that his children will be a people set apart for God.

Those people come from his grandson, Jacob. Jacob was a rather sinful man, lying to his father, cheating his brother out of an inheritance, yet as Paul said, "where sin abounds grace much more abounds" (Romans 5:20). So God still made a covenant with Jacob and made a nation out of him despite his deeds.

Another man, loved by God and said to have his own heart (1 Samuel 13:14), David has an illicit relationship with Bathsheba. Though the first child conceived in sin died, the second child, Solomon, succeeded David and built the temple of God. He brought fame of God's glory and wisdom throughout the entire world. Satan once again was made a fool of by God's abounding love for his creation and man reciprocating that love. David knew God, loved his law and had a heart after Him, so God called him to something greater.

Notes:
Then he said, "Your name shall no longer be called Jacob, but Israel, for you have striven with God and with men, and have prevailed."
    - Genesis 32:28 ESV

The name Jacob means "one who grasps the heel" or in our terminology "pulling your leg", or liar. Then when Jacob sought forgiveness and wrestled with God, his name was changed to Israel "struggles with God"; meaning despite fear or opposition, he would seek with everything until God was found.

He saw that there was no man, and wondered that there was no one to intercede; then his own arm brought him salvation, and his righteousness upheld him. - Isaiah 59:16 ESV

And we know that for those who love God all things work together for good, for those who are called according to his purpose.
    - Romans 8:28 ESV

John the Baptist foretells Jesus purpose and prepares the Jews for his coming saying ""You brood of vipers! Who warned you to flee from the wrath to come? 8 Bear fruit in keeping with repentance. 9 And do not presume to say to yourselves, 'We have Abraham as our father,' for I tell you, God is able from these stones to raise up children for Abraham. 10 Even now the axe is laid to the root of the trees. Every tree therefore that does not bear good fruit is cut down and thrown into the fire."
    - Matthew 3:7-10 ESV

For three years Jesus walked with his disciples as God walked with Adam, but then told them about the Spirit abiding with them in John chapter 16, and explains his heart and purpose for coming in his prayer. "20 "I do not ask for these only, but also for those who will believe in me through their word, 21 that they may all be one, just as you, Father, are in me, and I in you, that they also may be in us, so that the world may believe that you have sent me. 22 The glory that you have given me I have given to them, that they may be one even as we are one, 23 I in them and you in me, that they may become perfectly one, so that the world may know that you sent me and loved them even as you loved me." - .John 17:20-23 ESV

The Pharisees were the religious leaders or moral compass for Israel, and Jesus describes how prideful they are in a certain parable and says that they are of their father the devil, meaning they mimic him rather than God.

Time and time again, God thwarts the devil's plans. Satan tried to defame God's promise with Israel by destroying the deliverer Moses. Satan tried to destroy Israel with curses from Balaam, but they turned to blessings. Satan tried to destroy Israel by inciting Saul to sin against God and kill David who would be the ancestor of Christ. Eventually the nation of Israel runs out of people who remember why they were called by God: the devotion their father, Abraham, showed and God's love for him. This is the reason he bore with them; never gave up on them. He allowed them to be captured when they turned away and took his hand of protection from them, but always left a remnant. He raised prophets up to remind them of God's love and desire for them. They were all killed. History repeated itself. God knew it would happen eventually. He spoke of it through the prophet Isaiah. So he saved them by his own arm, or by his own Son. Just when Satan thought he had won, God brings his very self to mankind's aid. In panic he tries to kill the savior by inciting King Herod to kill all the babes at the time of Jesus' birth. Satan has always tried to destroy the relationship between God and man and tarnish God's character. He's never successful. Instead all things work together for the good of those who love God and are called according to his purpose. Jesus survives and gives the last warning call for Israel, basically saying "Repent, because you will no longer be my people. I will invite everyone to be in Abraham's lineage. They will inherit the promise. Whoever has that same heart and character, whoever has a desire to know me will be called a son of Abraham. I will honor their obedience and their faith."

Now we have the ability to have a relationship greater than that of Adam's. We can do more than walk with him, we can be in him just as the Son is in the Father. We no longer are just a copy of him, but we take part in him. Satan can't change what has happened, but he can try to keep us from fulfilling God's purpose. He allows us to be tempted in the same way the Israelites were, thinking we are entitled and able to live "good" lives unlike non-believers. He causes us to focus on doing good deeds and tells us "build your pride and

Notes:

He also told this parable to some who trusted in themselves that they were righteous, and treated others with contempt: 10 "Two men went up into the temple to pray, one a Pharisee and the other a tax collector. 11 The Pharisee, standing by himself, prayed thus: 'God, I thank you that I am not like other men, extortioners, unjust, adulterers, or even like this tax collector. 12 I fast twice a week; I give tithes of all that I get.' 13 But the tax collector, standing far off, would not even lift up his eyes to heaven, but beat his breast, saying, 'God, be merciful to me, a sinner!' 14 I tell you, this man went down to his house justified, rather than the other. For everyone who exalts himself will be humbled, but the one who humbles himself will be exalted." - Luke 18:9-14 ESV

You belong to your father, the devil, and you want to carry out your father's desire. He was a murderer from the beginning, not holding to the truth, for there is no truth in him. When he lies, he speaks his native language, for he is a liar and the father of lies. - John 8:44 NIV

As Jesus started on his way, a man ran up to him and fell on his knees before him. "Good teacher," he asked, "what must I do to inherit eternal life?" 18 "Why do you call me good?" Jesus answered. "No one is good--except God alone. 19 You know the commandments: 'Do not murder, do not commit adultery, do not steal, do not give false testimony, do not defraud, honor your father and mother.' " 20 "Teacher," he declared, "all these I have kept since I was a boy." 21 Jesus looked at him and loved him. "One thing you lack," he said. "Go, sell everything you have and give to the poor, and you will have treasure in heaven. Then come, follow me." 22 At this the man's face fell. He went away sad, because he had great wealth. 23 Jesus looked around and said to his disciples, "How hard it is for the rich to enter the kingdom of God!" - Mark 10:17-23 NIV

The man was unable to die to himself. He did not understand the law. Jesus said loving God with all of your heart, soul, and strength, and loving your neighbor as yourself sums up the law. (Luke 10:27, Matthew 7:12) He who breaks one commandment, breaks all of them (James 2:10). Because it is all about self-sacrificing love.

worth by yourself, try to get rich, know that you should be blessed with things of intrinsic value." So Christians pride themselves on their good deeds, but have forgotten how to truly love. They focus on getting things from God. They delude themselves into thinking we need revival because other people are corrupt and disobedient and evil. They say others need God, but in actuality they just want the people to act nicer and don't realize their own need for God. Revival is not about good deeds. Revive means to bring back to life. God wants to breathe into the church the life of his Holy Spirit. He wants us in Him, not good deeds. Isaiah said that our good deeds are but filthy rags. Paul says that we are saved by grace through faith, and that not even of ourselves lest we should boast. It is about us being united with God and carrying out his will, NOT good deeds.

It is interesting to note, a rich man came to Jesus and said, "Teacher, what good thing must I do to inherit eternal life?" To which Jesus replied, "Why do ask me about what is good? There is only One who is good." Even Jesus himself did not concern himself with or think of himself as "good". All the works of God in Genesis were "good". Everything goes to Him and portrays his character. Yet this is not all for his glory and to show how great He is, it is to show us and all creation how He loves. Jesus basically tells the man, love the poor as much as yourself. The "good" we must do is love. True love originates from God.

Notes:

"Say to the people of Israel, Any one of the people of Israel or of the strangers who sojourn in Israel who gives any of his children to Molech shall surely be put to death. The people of the land shall stone him with stones. - Leviticus 20:2 ESV

What then shall we say? That the law is sin? By no means! Yet if it had not been for the law, I would not have known sin. For I would not have known what it is to covet if the law had not said, "You shall not covet."
    - Romans 7:7 ESV

The Lord is not slow to fulfill his promise as some count slowness, but is patient toward you, not wishing that any should perish, but that all should reach repentance. - 2 Peter 3:9 ESV

He saw that there was no man, and wondered that there was no one to intercede; then his own arm brought him salvation, and his righteousness upheld him. - Isaiah 59:16 ESV

Did that which is good, then, bring death to me? By no means! It was sin, producing death in me through what is good, in order that sin might be shown to be sin, and through the commandment might become sinful beyond measure. - Romans 7:13 ESV

O Jerusalem, Jerusalem, the city that kills the prophets and stones those who are sent to it! How often would I have gathered your children together as a hen gathers her brood under her wings, and you would not!
    - Luke 13:34 ESV

And you, Capernaum, will you be exalted to heaven? You will be brought down to Hades. For if the mighty works done in you had been done in Sodom, it would have remained until this day. - Matthew 11:23 ESV

CHAPTER 2

GOD'S DESIGN

Many think that the Old Testament God is a God of wrath, but that's because his Son wasn't able to save man yet. So He had to get rid of the evil that was in the world. That's why He had the nation of Israel kill off their enemies, it was to keep them from being corrupted. These people were thoroughly evil, not just acting out in drunken violence, or theft, but having sex with children, sacrificing their kids to pagan gods, and sodomy. God even killed off some of his own people. He wanted a remnant of people that desired to seek his face. You may wonder, why then did God not send his Son first thing and keep everyone from dying? So we could see our need for him. Paul said, "How would I know I had sin without the law? It had to prove that I was exceedingly sinful." He tried sending prophets, and not just to Israel, Nineveh wasn't even a part of Israel. He had mercy on everyone who was willing to repent. God was always patient with us and still is, which is why Jesus hasn't come again. He always wanted us to take part with Him. But a time came when no one would listen, and so He had to save the world by "his own arm". Meaning his Son. It wasn't just all for Him, it was for us. He wants us to love one another. He doesn't just allow evil to continue, but He does try to juxtapose that evil to his goodness that we would see his mercy and come willingly to Him and know Him. It's been an invitation.

God, even when angry with his people, always had mercy and

Notes:

Abram settled in the land of Canaan, while Lot settled among the cities of the valley and moved his tent as far as Sodom. 13 Now the men of Sodom were wicked, great sinners against the LORD. - Genesis 13:12-13 ESV

God looked for someone to bridge the gap. He looked for people he could speak through to teach repentance. Abraham told him to look harder, look for 50 righteous people and went down to ten. God could not find any.

And the LORD replied, "If I find fifty innocent people in Sodom, I will spare the entire city for their sake."...32 Finally, Abraham said, "Lord, please do not get angry; I will speak but once more! Suppose only ten are found there?"And the LORD said, "Then, for the sake of the ten, I will not destroy it." - Genesis 18:26, 32 NLT

There was a similar city called Nineveh that was thoroughly evil, but God used Jonah to preach repentance and that city was spared.

There were laws put in place to keep people healthy. God told people what to do in case there was mold in the house, skin infections, diet, etc. (Leviticus Chapter 14) Things that took place because of the curse put on creation, he told them how to fix it or bypass it.

There were also laws that were civil ensuring everyone would be taken care of, children would take care of parents in their old age, extortion was outlawed, fruit and grain that fell from the trees were left over for the poor and even the animals that were treading the grain. (Mark 7:9-13, Leviticus 6:1-5, Deuteronomy 24:5)

But now your kingdom will not endure; the LORD has sought out a man after his own heart and appointed him leader of his people, because you have not kept the LORD's command." - 1 Samuel 13:14 NIV

At midnight I rise to give you thanks for your righteous laws.
    - Psalm 119:62 NIV

compassion. Jesus said God wanted to gather his children under his wings like a hen gathers her chicks. His people weren't willing. Jesus said that his people were so obstinate, the miracles that he performed for them, if Sodom and Gomorrah saw them, they would've repented, but Capernaum did not. So you would think "then why did God destroy that nation?". Lot seemed righteous, but was drawn to that city, and even his wife had attachment to it. But it was the sin and wickedness they loved. God said that He could not find anyone righteous in that city, but told Abraham for the sake of him and the love he had for his family he would get Lot out of there. God is always patient, but like I said he wanted someone to take action, someone to use that had his zeal for holiness, because holiness is actually jealous love. It is love that protects.

Compare it to an ant you see in the kitchen. One ant does little damage, but allow it to live and that ant will bring hundreds back with it. You have to destroy the one ant and every trace of him (the pheromone trail) so they do not overrun the house. The same thing pertains to sin and holiness. For this reason God destroyed everything that belonged to the pagans that the Israelites conquered. However, He did allow the people that repented and the allies with Israel to live (e.g. Rahab).

So this explains how the war and violence is out of love. But what about the law and all the ceremonies and regulations? God set those in place for love too. Some laws taught the men holiness and helped them understand God's perspective. Others ensured people treated one another fairly. Others took it as a right to be vindictive and require payment from someone if they were wronged. God tried to show his heart to a people that could not understand. So He gave specific rules to try to lead them to righteousness and love. There were laws about canceling debt after so many years. It was to show mercy to their brothers. Everything was based off the character of God. David had a certain understanding of it and praised God. If you read Psalm 119 you will see how he raves about God's law and the greatness of his wisdom and understanding. He was said to have the heart of God, and this is why he praised God in the midnight watches, he truly understood the character of God. Because of this

Notes:

The pig is also unclean; although it has a split hoof, it does not chew the cud. You are not to eat their meat or touch their carcasses.
- Deuteronomy 14:8 NIV

The judges must make a thorough investigation, and if the witness proves to be a liar, giving false testimony against his brother, 19 then do to him as he intended to do to his brother. You must purge the evil from among you. 20 The rest of the people will hear of this and be afraid, and never again will such an evil thing be done among you. 21 Show no pity: life for life, eye for eye, tooth for tooth, hand for hand, foot for foot.
- Deuteronomy 19:18-21 NIV

Do not be misled: "Bad company corrupts good character."
- 1 Corinthians 15:33 NIV

Paul said this in regards to a prideful church that had a man engage in sexual immorality. He was concerned that a people not zealous for holiness would be easily corrupted by another's sin. "Your boasting is not good. Don't you know that a little yeast works through the whole batch of dough?" - 1 Corinthians 5:6 NIV

And do not neglect the Levites living in your towns, for they have no allotment or inheritance of their own. 28 At the end of every three years, bring all the tithes of that year's produce and store it in your towns, 29 so that the Levites (who have no allotment or inheritance of their own) and the aliens, the fatherless and the widows who live in your towns may come and eat and be satisfied, and so that the LORD your God may bless you in all the work of your hands. - Deuteronomy 14:27-29 NIV

God wanted Jesus to be in David's line.

God's grand design has been to share with us his glory and share in his love. He used every attack of the devil and every downfall of man as the perfect stage to show his grace. However, there is plenty of judgment. God judges hearts, not actions. He wrote the law through Moses to try to show people what love was and also to protect them from the curse that fell upon the earth. He tried to keep them from pestilence. Right now it seems absurd to hurt someone for touching a pig skin, which atheists love to bring up. A pig was an unclean animal, still is, ain't a healthy animal, and it has parasites. God wanted to protect his people from sickness and disease. He knew that we are like children and if we don't have a clear cut boundary we'd hold our finger an inch from that pig and chant "I'm not touching it, I'm not touching it." He also wanted fairness, thus the "eye for an eye". He did not want the people to try to vindicate themselves, he tried explaining The Golden Rule to a childish people. Like saying to a toddler, "Tommy, do you like it when Billy kicks you in the leg?" When I was a kid I would always try to find loop holes. "If I can't have candy now, can I have it tomorrow?" Or when asked if I brushed my teeth, I would say yes. Then my mom learned to tack on "today?" No. That's how we are, and that's why the law is long and in-depth. Israel was an obstinate people, and they memorized the law at an early age, no one was ignorant. If they disobeyed, they more than likely did it on purpose. The punishment was often harsh because God knew "bad company corrupts good character." Meaning evil easily creeps in and overtakes like yeast. That's why it was written "purge the evil from among you".

God knew people needed to provide for themselves and have jobs and cattle and fields and trades, so He made sure they had a livelihood. However, He also wanted to make sure no one forgot Him in the midst of them working, so He made one tribe completely devoted to Him. The Levites took care of Israel spiritually, and the rest of the people took care of the Levites with their tithe.

Once the ark of the covenant was touched by someone who was

Notes:

When they came to the threshing floor of Kidon, Uzzah reached out his hand to steady the ark, because the oxen stumbled. 10 The LORD's anger burned against Uzzah, and he struck him down because he had put his hand on the ark. So he died there before God. - 1 Chronicles 13:9-10 NIV

This seems harsh, but once again this was no accident. Uzzah knew the power of God, had seen many miracles and knew that he was not a false god nor man-made idol that cannot take care of himself, this man presumed himself to be good enough to touch the ark. Being familiar with God's law the man knew better.

I know your deeds, that you are neither cold nor hot. I wish you were either one or the other! 16 So, because you are lukewarm--neither hot nor cold--I am about to spit you out of my mouth. - Revelation 3:15-16 NIV

not a priest and he fell down dead. That may seem harsh, but God had strict rules concerning the ark. The ark held his presence and God is holy. Only those who were clean levitical priests could touch the ark. It was not out of pride, but for the people's safety. A man cannot be divided and touch God. A good example is a power line. If you stand on the ground and touch a power line with a pole you get killed. You are touching the ground and the wire at the same time. If you hang from a power line you are fine, because you are not grounded. You cannot be of the world and of God at the same time. God said "I wish you were hot or cold, but because you are lukewarm I will spew you out of my mouth." If we are to be in God we must be holy.

Notes:

You hypocrites! Isaiah was right when he prophesied about you: 8 " 'These people honor me with their lips, but their hearts are far from me. 9 They worship me in vain; their teachings are but rules taught by men.'"
    - Matthew 15:7-9 NIV

"You snakes! You brood of vipers! How will you escape being condemned to hell? - Matthew 23:33 NIV

"Woe to you, teachers of the law and Pharisees, you hypocrites! You give a tenth of your spices--mint, dill and cummin. But you have neglected the more important matters of the law--justice, mercy and faithfulness. You should have practiced the latter, without neglecting the former.
    - Matthew 23:23 NIV

Going on from that place, he went into their synagogue, 10 and a man with a shriveled hand was there. Looking for a reason to accuse Jesus, they asked him, "Is it lawful to heal on the Sabbath?" 11 He said to them, "If any of you has a sheep and it falls into a pit on the Sabbath, will you not take hold of it and lift it out? 12 How much more valuable is a man than a sheep! Therefore it is lawful to do good on the Sabbath." - Matthew 12:9-12 NIV

Then he said to them, "The Sabbath was made for man, not man for the Sabbath. - Mark 2:27 NIV

Calling his disciples to him, Jesus said, "I tell you the truth, this poor widow has put more into the treasury than all the others. 44 They all gave out of their wealth; but she, out of her poverty, put in everything--all she had to live on." - Mark 12:43-44 NIV

CHAPTER 3

WHEN AND WHY

JESUS CAME

The teachers of the law did not have an understanding of the law. They desired to be righteous and appear holy, but they were condemned by Christ. He said Isaiah was right when he prophesied about them, that they did little more than lip-service. Jesus said that they neglected more important matters of the law: justice and mercy.

Jesus did things that seemed contrary to the law because he did things differently than the Pharisees. He didn't follow the law to the "T". Then again they didn't get the context in which the rules were set. The most important aspect of the law is the definition of terms, or how the law is to be interpreted. The Pharisees thought it was wrong to work at all on the Sabbath. Jesus knew the context was to rest from your worldly cares and stop working to provide for one day, or to not concern one's self with riches. But a labor of love, that was allowed on the Sabbath. And Jesus did just that. He did God's work showing love and healing on the Sabbath. Jesus brought the law into perspective.

When Jesus saw men giving large sums of money to the temple he was not impressed. When he saw a woman give a penny, he was

Notes:

All the believers were together and had everything in common. 45 Selling their possessions and goods, they gave to anyone as he had need.
    - Acts 2:44-45 NIV

At the end of every three years, bring all the tithes of that year's produce and store it in your towns, 29 so that the Levites (who have no allotment or inheritance of their own) and the aliens, the fatherless and the widows who live in your towns may come and eat and be satisfied, and so that the LORD your God may bless you in all the work of your hands.
    - Deuteronomy 14:28-29 NIV

"Will a man rob God? Yet you rob me. "But you ask, 'How do we rob you?' "In tithes and offerings. 9 You are under a curse--the whole nation of you-- because you are robbing me. 10 Bring the whole tithe into the storehouse, that there may be food in my house. Test me in this," says the LORD Almighty, "and see if I will not throw open the floodgates of heaven and pour out so much blessing that you will not have room enough for it.
    - Malachi 3:8-10 NIV

God is obviously not in need of our money. All he wants is for us to love.

"If I were hungry I would not tell you, for the world is mine, and all that is in it." -Psalms 50:12 NIV

When I heard their outcry and these charges, I was very angry. 7 I pondered them in my mind and then accused the nobles and officials. I told them, "You are exacting usury from your own countrymen!" So I called together a large meeting to deal with them 8 and said: "As far as possible, we have bought back our Jewish brothers who were sold to the Gentiles. Now you are selling your brothers, only for them to be sold back to us!" They kept quiet, because they could find nothing to say. - Nehemiah 5:6-8 NIV

moved because she gave everything she had. She was focused on God more than her own livelihood. The disciples took note of this and lived by the spirit of the law sharing everything they had in common so that no one would be without. Which is really what the tithe was for. The levitical priests had no other wages than the other tribes giving their tithe. God wanted to make sure that the men that were devoted to his work would receive compensation. The other tribes robbed God in that they did not provide for their brothers in the book of Malachi. The tithe is not giving to an organization, but to people. They did the same thing in Nehemiah, and Nehemiah scolded them for not having mercy on their brothers.

Why Jesus Died

Many don't understand why Jesus died. We just accept that He died for sins and take it at face value. When you think about it, it doesn't make much sense. Jesus died for sins, but then he came back to life. If he bore our punishment, and the punishment for sin is death, he wasn't dead for very long. And if his death was a sacrifice, a sacrifice is usually something you can't get back. The priest didn't offer a lamb, cut it to pieces, burn it, then bring it back to life like a magician. That lamb was gone forever. How was Jesus' temporary death a sacrifice? It wasn't even like Abraham and Isaac. Abraham had to trust God to perform his promise. God Himself, though, is sacrificing his own Son. They both already know the outcome. This isn't a test either. How does it mean anything? Because, Adam had fellowship with God and fell away from that fellowship as a result of sin and that sin was laid upon all of his children. God had to reverse that. So He took a man who had never sinned, his own Son, and laid all the sin upon Him. He broke the fellowship with his Son. That had never happened since before the beginning of time. This is why Jesus feared and sweat blood. He had reason to fear. Because his peace in the fellowship with God was shaken, yet he still trusted even when separated from God. That is why he died. He died physically and spiritually, and conquered that death and rose again. That is why Paul says there would be no hope without the resurrection. He conquered the spiritual death we all had. Death is separation, either us from God or the spirit from the body. Death is a separation.

Notes:

But Christ has indeed been raised from the dead, the firstfruits of those who have fallen asleep. 21 For since death came through a man, the resurrection of the dead comes also through a man. 22 For as in Adam all die, so in Christ all will be made alive. 23 But each in his own turn: Christ, the firstfruits; then, when he comes, those who belong to him. 24 Then the end will come, when he hands over the kingdom to God the Father after he has destroyed all dominion, authority and power. 25 For he must reign until he has put all his enemies under his feet. 26 The last enemy to be destroyed is death... 55 "Where, O death, is your victory? Where, O death, is your sting?" 56 The sting of death is sin, and the power of sin is the law. 57 But thanks be to God! He gives us the victory through our Lord Jesus Christ.
- 1 Corinthians 15:20-26, 55-57 NIV

the LORD God formed the man from the dust of the ground and breathed into his nostrils the breath of life, and the man became a living being.
- Genesis 2:7 NIV

Again Jesus said, "Peace be with you! As the Father has sent me, I am sending you." 22 And with that he breathed on them and said, "Receive the Holy Spirit. - John 20:21-22 NIV

Therefore, if anyone is in Christ, he is a new creation; the old has gone, the new has come! - 2 Corinthians 5:17 NIV

Jesus brought back what had been separated. He allowed for us to have fellowship and even that greater than Adam's. We were formed in the image of Adam, we were sons of Adam. Now we are sons of God joined together with, and in, Christ. This then becomes Jesus departing message to the disciples, "peace I give to you" and then he breathed into them new life. He breathed on them and they received the Holy Spirit. Remember how Adam was formed; God breathed into him the breath of life. Jesus breathed into the disciples new life. This is why we are a "new creation". We have been recreated.

Notes:

Many times we think God does not answer us, but it's not that he's ignoring us, we are ignoring him. Look at how the Jesus responds to the Pharisees questions.

Jesus entered the temple courts, and, while he was teaching, the chief priests and the elders of the people came to him. "By what authority are you doing these things?" they asked. "And who gave you this authority?" 24 Jesus replied, "I will also ask you one question. If you answer me, I will tell you by what authority I am doing these things. 25 John's baptism--where did it come from? Was it from heaven, or from men?" They discussed it among themselves and said, "If we say, 'From heaven,' he will ask, 'Then why didn't you believe him?' 26 But if we say, 'From men'--we are afraid of the people, for they all hold that John was a prophet." 27 So they answered Jesus, "We don't know." Then he said, "Neither will I tell you by what authority I am doing these things. - Matthew 21:23-27 NIV

They wouldn't have accepted his answer even if he told them...because he did tell them numerous times. God wants to tell us why, we just need our ears open.

Joshua asks something similar to what is written to the right.

CHAPTER 4

PRAYER -

HEART TO HEART

When talking about God answering prayer, people love to use the cliché: It's one of three things, yes, no, or wait. That's not the greatest definition. I think God often answers our questions with another question. If something doesn't happen within 24hrs He's asking you, "Why do you want that?" For instance if you want to see some miracle like someone rising from the dead or getting out of a wheelchair you would say, "God do it so you will be glorified." God doesn't do it.

"Why not God?"

"Well, you said you would like to see it for my glory, is that true?"

"Of course it is God, I want your fame to spread throughout the earth."

"That's very noble of you. So it's not for your fame?"

"Oh no, God not at all, only you can do this sort of miracle, I don't plan on healing all the time."

"Really? You know that's what my son did after he was baptized right up until his death"

"Um... well, you know I have a job, and kids and I just like part-time ministry."

"So you just want me to heal this once so you can say you saw a

Notes:

And Joshua said, "Ah, Sovereign LORD, why did you ever bring this people across the Jordan to deliver us into the hands of the Amorites to destroy us? If only we had been content to stay on the other side of the Jordan! 8 O Lord, what can I say, now that Israel has been routed by its enemies? 9 The Canaanites and the other people of the country will hear about this and they will surround us and wipe out our name from the earth. What then will you do for your own great name?" 10 The LORD said to Joshua, "Stand up! What are you doing down on your face? 11 Israel has sinned; they have violated my covenant, which I commanded them to keep. They have taken some of the devoted things; they have stolen, they have lied, they have put them with their own possessions. 12 That is why the Israelites cannot stand against their enemies; they turn their backs and run because they have been made liable to destruction. I will not be with you anymore unless you destroy whatever among you is devoted to destruction. 13 "Go, consecrate the people. Tell them, 'Consecrate yourselves in preparation for tomorrow; for this is what the LORD, the God of Israel, says: That which is devoted is among you, O Israel. You cannot stand against your enemies until you remove it. - Joshua 7:7-13 NIV

And the LORD told him: "Listen to all that the people are saying to you; it is not you they have rejected, but they have rejected me as their king. 8 As they have done from the day I brought them up out of Egypt until this day, forsaking me and serving other gods, so they are doing to you.
    - 1 Samuel 8:7-8 NIV

Jesus tells the people not to worry about how they are viewed or what others think about their spirituality. Be more concerned about God and having time with him alone. Do not think the number of words you say has any bearing on whether God perceives you as earnest. He already knows your heart.

time where I worked when someone criticizes you for believing in a God that does not heal."

"UM sort of... I guess."

"So it's not really because you love the person that you want to see them made whole, and it's not for my glory, it's more or less so you don't look stupid in front of other people when you profess to be a Christian and have no answer for them when they ask you for a miracle."

" cough*"

At times we worry about being a failure in front of others, or failing God by not showing his power. We focus on our selves and not him. God is not glorified through just a display of miracles. He wants people to see his character, not his power. He already made the earth, we know his power. We don't know Him. This is what prayer is for. Communication is about receiving information, not objects. Christians often pray for things, but not for God. Even when praying for revival we pray for things. Revival does not consist of miracles, it consists of us being revived by God's Spirit and miracles follow. We pursue God's heart and become one with Him in order to see his will done on earth as it is in heaven.

Let me explain the Lord's Prayer:

Our Father who is in heaven:	God you are not a stranger, but my Father full of love and character, and I'm your child
Hallowed be your name:	Please may what I do and say truly reflect your character, don't let me dishonor you
Your Kingdom come your will be done:	Your kingdom is in my heart, may it be pure and right before you
On Earth as it is in Heaven:	So that you can use me in showing those on earth who you are
Give us this day our daily bread:	Provide me what I need BOTH physically and spiritually

Notes:

"And when you pray, do not be like the hypocrites, for they love to pray standing in the synagogues and on the street corners to be seen by men. I tell you the truth, they have received their reward in full. 6 But when you pray, go into your room, close the door and pray to your Father, who is unseen. Then your Father, who sees what is done in secret, will reward you. 7 And when you pray, do not keep on babbling like pagans, for they think they will be heard because of their many words. 8 Do not be like them, for your Father knows what you need before you ask him. 9 "This, then, is how you should pray: " 'Our Father in heaven, hallowed be your name, 10 your kingdom come, your will be done on earth as it is in heaven. 11 Give us today our daily bread. 12 Forgive us our debts, as we also have forgiven our debtors. 13 And lead us not into temptation, but deliver us from the evil one. ' - Matthew 6:5-11 NIV

Jesus says he is the bread of life. John says that Jesus is the Word. Jesus says his nourishment is doing the will of God. Daily bread is God giving us himself to sustain us.

If you abide in Me, and My words abide in you, you will ask what you desire, and it shall be done for you. - John 15:7 NKJV

You ask and do not receive, because you ask amiss, that you may spend it on your pleasures. - James 4:3 NKJV

So in everything, do to others what you would have them do to you, for this sums up the Law and the Prophets. - Matthew 7:12 NIV

Jesus replied: " 'Love the Lord your God with all your heart and with all your soul and with all your mind.' 38 This is the first and greatest commandment. 39 And the second is like it: 'Love your neighbor as yourself.' 40 All the Law and the Prophets hang on these two commandments." - Matthew 22:37-40 NIV

"Therefore, if you are offering your gift at the altar and there remember that your brother has something against you, 24 leave your gift there in front of the altar. First go and be reconciled to your brother; then come and offer your gift. - Matthew 5:23-24 NIV

Forgive us our sins as we forgive others:	Make sure I'm not bitter towards anyone so as to separate myself from you
And lead us not into temptation:	please do not give me more than I can handle, whether I want it or not
But deliver us from the evil one:	help me cast down all these fears that I get and keep my trust in you
For yours is the Kingdom and the glory and the power forever:	Because I am yours, and you are great and powerful and always faithful.

Jesus says if we abide in him and his words in us we will receive whatever we ask for. James tells us the reason we don't receive is because we ask in selfishness. Remember Jesus saying "Do unto others as you would have them do to you, for this sums of the law and the prophets"? He just wanted us to love, so if the Bible is pretty much "the law and the prophets", if we love God and others and have them in mind when asking for what we desire, then we will receive whatever we ask for in prayer.

There's something still missing though. Jesus says if we present an offering and remember our brother has something against us, first go and be reconciled to your brother and then offer your gift. John says that we cannot claim to be of God if we have hatred toward our brother. So when making a request we have to forgive others and get rid of all bitterness.

The best way to pray is to ask for more of God and not things. "Lord, instead of granting my family money, give them wisdom in how to use money. You said everyone who has will be given more, and if we are faithful with a little you could trust us with much. God this issue needs to be fixed, please give them wisdom. You said if anyone lacks it we could ask and that you give liberally to everyone without finding fault." You see, Jesus' sermon on the mount teaches us that God knows our needs before we ask and that He is a good Father knowing how to give good gifts to his children. To doubt

Notes:

Anyone who claims to be in the light but hates his brother is still in the darkness. - 1 John 2:9 NIV

Directly after the Lord's Prayer, Jesus says this. "For if you forgive men when they sin against you, your heavenly Father will also forgive you. But if you do not forgive men their sins, your Father will not forgive your sins."
    - Matthew 6:14-15 NIV

"Which of you fathers, if your son asks for a fish, will give him a snake instead? 12 Or if he asks for an egg, will give him a scorpion? 13 If you then, though you are evil, know how to give good gifts to your children, how much more will your Father in heaven give the Holy Spirit to those who ask him!" - Luke 11:11-13 NIV

So give your servant a discerning heart to govern your people and to distinguish between right and wrong. For who is able to govern this great people of yours?" 10 The Lord was pleased that Solomon had asked for this. 11 So God said to him, "Since you have asked for this and not for long life or wealth for yourself, nor have asked for the death of your enemies but for discernment in administering justice, 12 I will do what you have asked. I will give you a wise and discerning heart, so that there will never have been anyone like you, nor will there ever be. 13 Moreover, I will give you what you have not asked for--both riches and honor--so that in your lifetime you will have no equal among kings. 14 And if you walk in my ways and obey my statutes and commands as David your father did, I will give you a long life." - 1 Kings 3:9-14 NIV

One thing I ask of the LORD, this is what I seek: that I may dwell in the house of the LORD all the days of my life, to gaze upon the beauty of the LORD and to seek him in his temple. - Psalm 27:4 NIV

Delight yourself in the LORD and he will give you the desires of your heart. - Psalm 37:4 NIV

O LORD, you have searched me and you know me. 2 You know when I sit and when I rise; you perceive my thoughts from afar. 3 You discern my going out and my lying down; you are familiar with all my ways. 4 Before a word is on my tongue you know it completely, O LORD. 5 You hem me in--behind and before; you have laid your hand upon me. 6 Such knowledge is too wonderful for me, too lofty for me to attain. - Psalms 139:1-6 NIV

God's provision would be to doubt his very character. We need his character.

Remember the man who asked for wisdom? Solomon asked for wisdom above everything else, and wisdom to benefit the nation of Israel and not himself. God saw this request as most noble and granted him everything, from wealth, to prestige, power, and fame. Solomon's father, David, inquired of God himself. He studied the law, praised God for his understanding, and what was his request? Just to seek God and dwell in his house every moment of every day. What is God going to withhold from that man? Delight yourself in the LORD, and He will grant you your heart's desires. If we were to just fulfill our purpose in seeking out God, we wouldn't have to chase our dreams. They'd fall in our lap, and we could actually enjoy them. I say that because, Solomon in all of his splendor, attaining everything you could ever want in life, saw that all was meaningless without God. It's really all about Him, because everything else passes away.

When you talk to someone you care about, do you make the conversation about you? Or do you ask questions about them? Do you comprehend who you are talking to when you pray? This man knows every thought, every word you are about to say, your every move, and knows every detail about the world at any given second. He even knows how fast you are losing your hair. Taking all that into account, what do you say? "Let me shut up and listen to you!" Not to say you shouldn't speak at all, but just emphasizing the importance of listening. After understanding Him, the greatest prayer would sound like "God teach me your love and how to show it to others in every action I make today."

Let me tell you how to listen, because too many people don't know how to listen. We are used to half listening in the natural and know little to nothing regarding listening in the spiritual. Typically when we listen for God, we want to hear him say something. Wanting to hear something is not the same as listening. A gossiper wants to hear "something" but that doesn't mean they are listening intently. So whatever we think we hear, we go off on and say we have a word from God that may or may not be right. If you are having trouble hearing, listen to what he has already said. "I don't utter vain obscurities", "My sheep know my voice", "Blessed are your

Notes:

I publicly proclaim bold promises. I do not whisper obscurities in some dark corner so no one can understand what I mean. And I did not tell the people of Israel to ask me for something I did not plan to give. I, the LORD, speak only what is true and right. - Isaiah 45:19 NLT

I did not speak in secret, in a land of darkness; I did not say to the offspring of Jacob, 'Seek me in vain.' I the LORD speak the truth; I declare what is right. - Isaiah 45:19 ESV

My sheep recognize my voice; I know them, and they follow me.
    - John 10:27 NLT

He replied, "The knowledge of the secrets of the kingdom of heaven has been given to you, but not to them... 16 But blessed are your eyes because they see, and your ears because they hear. - Matthew 13:11,16 NIV

However, as it is written: "No eye has seen, no ear has heard, no mind has conceived what God has prepared for those who love him"-- 10 but God has revealed it to us by his Spirit. The Spirit searches all things, even the deep things of God. 11 For who among men knows the thoughts of a man except the man's spirit within him? In the same way no one knows the thoughts of God except the Spirit of God. 12 We have not received the spirit of the world but the Spirit who is from God, that we may understand what God has freely given us. - 1 Corinthians 2:9-12 NIV

ears because they hear", "We have received the Spirit who is from God." You don't have to guess at which voice is God's. He gives you certainty. So just take a moment and rest knowing that he wants you to hear and you are capable of hearing with certainty. When you get to know someone, a friend or family, you have inside jokes, looks, expressions, that are only discernible between the two of you. And while everyone else is guessing trying to figure out what was just said, you know for certain what that person means. That's how God speaks to you. He reveals himself and you know for certain what he is saying when you come to him with all your heart, completely genuine.

Notes:

As far as I am concerned, God turned into good what you meant for evil. He brought me to the high position I have today so I could save the lives of many people. - Genesis 50:20 NLT

Many are the afflictions of the righteous, But the Lord delivers him out of them all. - Psalm 34:19 NKJV

When Job was afflicted his friends assumed it was because he was an evil person hiding his deeds from them. God showed them their reasoning was false, and then blessed Job even more than before.

Paul was a great minister because he could relate to all. He started out as a self-righteous Jew that literally had to be knocked of his high-horse, so he was able to relate to the religious. Then God showed him grace and Paul was able to share that with the Gentiles. Then Paul suffered nearly everything: starvation, nakedness, imprisonment, being stoned within an inch of his life, but saw in every affliction he gained something for the gospel's sake.

For though I am free from all men, I have made myself a servant to all, that I might win the more; 20 and to the Jews I became as a Jew, that I might win Jews; to those who are under the law, as under the law, that I might win those who are under the law; 21 to those who are without law, as without law (not being without law toward God, but under law toward Christ), that I might win those who are without law; 22 to the weak I became as weak, that I might win the weak. I have become all things to all men, that I might by all means save some. 23 Now this I do for the gospel's sake, that I may be partaker of it with you. - 1 Corinthians 9:19-23 NKJV

CHAPTER 5

GOD IN

TIMES OF TROUBLE

Many will have lived a difficult life. I look at those that have been through sex trafficking and can't help but think what position they are in. "How is God good and faithful when he allows me to be sold into slavery?" But Joseph was. Joseph was a man sold into slavery by his own brothers, and later put in prison. How could God be faithful in all that? Yet God remained with him and Joseph did not become bitter, but desired to meet again with his brothers even after the betrayal. It's difficult to see what good could come of this. Girls sold into sex slavery don't become queens or vice-presidents. However it wasn't so Joseph would have power and honor, it was so he could save the lives of many people. There is some possibility that God can cause good to come from that sort of situation. Also, we have to remember there is an enemy, it's not just God that ordains bad things to happen.

Joseph rose to power after being buffeted by Satan, and then there was Job who fell from posterity to nothing, and then became twice as rich as before. God doesn't promise to keep us from trouble, He promises to deliver us out of trouble. We need Him. Some may not recognize their need because of riches, others will

Notes:

Are they ministers of Christ?--I speak as a fool--I am more: in labors more abundant, in stripes above measure, in prisons more frequently, in deaths often. 24 From the Jews five times I received forty stripes minus one. 25 Three times I was beaten with rods; once I was stoned; three times I was shipwrecked; a night and a day I have been in the deep; 26 in journeys often, in perils of waters, in perils of robbers, in perils of my own countrymen, in perils of the Gentiles, in perils in the city, in perils in the wilderness, in perils in the sea, in perils among false brethren; 27 in weariness and toil, in sleeplessness often, in hunger and thirst, in fastings often, in cold and nakedness-- 28 besides the other things, what comes upon me daily: my deep concern for all the churches. 29 Who is weak, and I am not weak? Who is made to stumble, and I do not burn with indignation? - 2 Corinthians: 11:23-29 NIV

I consider that our present sufferings are not worth comparing with the glory that will be revealed in us. - Romans 8:18 NIV

For this reason their hearts have become calloused. Though seeing they do not perceive, though hearing, they do not listen or understand. Lest they should see with their eyes, hear with their ears, and I would turn and heal them. - Isaiah 6:10 NIV

If my people, who are called by my name, will humble themselves and pray and seek my face and turn from their wicked ways, then will I hear from heaven and will forgive their sin and will heal their land.
     - 2 Chronicles 7:14 NIV

Jesus prophesied about the end times, "9 Then you will be handed over to be persecuted and put to death, and you will be hated by all nations because of me. 10 At that time many will turn away from the faith and will betray and hate each other, 11 and many false prophets will appear and deceive many people. 12 Because of the increase of wickedness, the love of most will grow cold, 13 but he who stands firm to the end will be saved."
     - Matthew 24:9-13 NIV

Bear one another's burdens, and so fulfill the law of Christ...9 And let us not grow weary while doing good, for in due season we shall reap if we do not lose heart. 10 Therefore, as we have opportunity, let us do good to all, especially to those who are of the household of faith.
     - Galatians 6:2, 9, 10 NIV

deny their need because of bitterness and pride. We may become angry because God didn't keep us from heartache and refuse Him. God can turn misfortune into great fortune. Jesus said that those who left houses or mothers or brothers or lands for his sake, would receive a hundred times as much in this age and the one to come. God restores what was lost.

Pain brings us perspective. We can live OK if we don't see others suffering, but when we suffer and see others suffer the same, we no longer pretend. We relate and love one another. If someone is willing to open up there is hope and healing. If they remain bitter and closed there is hopelessness. The world becomes unfeeling and cold.

Things happen, there is freewill and we are all affected by each other one way or another. There's no way around it. Someone has to be the catalyst and choose to receive from God and love others. Do not think that your decisions do not affect another person. I made mention of sex trafficking. You may think pornography is OK and you are not hurting anyone, but if you look you fund and promote the trafficking of women. Most are deceived or coerced into performing these acts. Very few, if any, do it out of their own free will. Search "Pink Cross Foundation" for more information. Even if you go to YouTube or DailyMotion or any video search engine the companies track it and use that information. People know. There is no secret sin.

Notes:

But he gives more grace. Therefore it says, "God opposes the proud, but gives grace to the humble." - James 4:6 ESV

The Pharisees asked for a sign and Jesus said, "No, every sign I give you is not good enough, but you will have no argument when I die and rise again." They accused him of driving out demons by the power of Satan. Then they asked by what authority he did miracles. He tested them regarding their own discernment and asked them where John the Baptist got his authority. They denied him being a prophet, mostly because he accused them of sinning. Jesus said the same thing. They didn't want to hear it. Those that were not self-righteous, but confessed their sin received healing. (James 5:16)

18 "The Spirit of the Lord is on me, because he has anointed me to preach good news to the poor. He has sent me to proclaim freedom for the prisoners and recovery of sight for the blind, to release the oppressed, 19 to proclaim the year of the Lord's favor." 20 Then he rolled up the scroll, gave it back to the attendant and sat down. The eyes of everyone in the synagogue were fastened on him, 21 and he began by saying to them, "Today this scripture is fulfilled in your hearing." - Luke 4:18-21 NIV

See to it that no one fails to obtain the grace of God; that no "root of bitterness" springs up and causes trouble, and by it many become defiled;
     - Hebrews 12:15 ESV

Therefore humble yourselves under the mighty hand of God, that He may exalt you in due time, 7 casting all your care upon Him, for He cares for you. 8 Be sober, be vigilant; because your adversary the devil walks about like a roaring lion, seeking whom he may devour. 9 Resist him, steadfast in the faith, knowing that the same sufferings are experienced by your brotherhood in the world. 10 But may the God of all grace, who called us to His eternal glory by Christ Jesus, after you have suffered a while, perfect, establish, strengthen, and settle you. - 1 Peter 5:6-10 NKJV

CHAPTER 6

A BROKEN HEART

God resists the proud but gives grace to the humble. Most haughtiness is caused by bitterness, whether you were hurt by somebody, or you just didn't get your way. For some reason though, people act better than others when they have insecurities. A home life might've been terrible with parents fighting and a child being abused. Then they shut everyone out and say people don't understand and they do their own thing, they are their own person, their own boss. The insecurity has to be dealt with before they can open up. God resists the proud because they are closed off, and gives grace when someone is open to him. When the Pharisees asked for the sign they were bitter because they didn't have what he had and they were considered the authority. He showed them they had none and they didn't want to hear it; they didn't want to see it. It was more or less a test for him to fail that they were asking for. They wanted a reason not to believe him. Those that wanted to believe him and receive him received miracles and healing from him. God desires to bind up the brokenhearted, he prophesied that about the Christ. He wanted to heal people so He could be near them. This is why we don't receive or understand.

It is extremely difficult to get to that place, because as soon as you open up Satan wants to make sure you never do it again. He nearly guarantees you will be hurt again. That's why people will open up to God and then be forever closed because they didn't see him as

Notes:

And without faith it is impossible to please him, for whoever would draw near to God must believe that he exists and that he rewards those who seek him. - Hebrews 11:6 ESV

When the servant of the man of God rose early in the morning and went out, behold, an army with horses and chariots was all around the city. And the servant said, "Alas, my master! What shall we do?" 16 He said, "Do not be afraid, for those who are with us are more than those who are with them." 17 Then Elisha prayed and said, "O LORD, please open his eyes that he may see." So the LORD opened the eyes of the young man, and he saw, and behold, the mountain was full of horses and chariots of fire all around Elisha. - 2 Kings 6:15-17 ESV

Indeed, in their case the prophecy of Isaiah is fulfilled that says: "'You will indeed hear but never understand, and you will indeed see but never perceive. 15 For this people's heart has grown dull, and with their ears they can barely hear, and their eyes they have closed, lest they should see with their eyes and hear with their ears and understand with their heart and turn, and I would heal them.' - Matthew 13:14-15 ESV

I call heaven and earth to witness against you today, that I have set before you life and death, blessing and curse. Therefore choose life, that you and your offspring may live, - Deuteronomy 30:19 ESV

soon as they opened up. I've done the same thing before. It's difficult when you want to embrace your wife and she is completely rigid, unable to open her hands or arms, you reach out to hold her and feel a cold, hard brace around her back. It's extremely difficult to count your blessings when you've got some sort of weakness dominating your life. It's hard to be thankful and receive anything from God when it looks like He's refusing your most dire request.

Satan wants you to focus on the negative and what hasn't been accomplished to ensure nothing more happens. We need to stop focusing on what God hasn't done and look at where we are missing it. He has character that we don't. "If anyone wants to come after God he must believe that he is and that he is a rewarder of those that diligently seek him." Ok, so God I am not feeling rewarded, where have I neglected you? Where does love not permeate? Where do I feel hopeless? I need faith, I need to see God before I can see a miracle. Elisha's servant saw an army surrounding him because he couldn't see God. Elisha could see God's hand right in the midst of trouble and instead of feeling hopeless, he felt confident in knowing that he was surrounded by angels. My greatest prayer has always been, "God open our eyes". Jesus reiterated Isaiah's words numerous times saying "though seeing they never perceive, otherwise they would see with their eyes." Our hearts too, have become calloused. We need to see God before we can see him operate.

I saw an extremely weird movie once, that was so artsy you had to meditate on what was going on, otherwise you'd just leave the movie and think the director was off his rocker. There was this man that made propositions to a great many people. He would go up to a couple and say, "If you open this box you will get millions of dollars, but someone you don't know will die as a result." The couple didn't see how someone could die from them just opening a wooden box with no electronics on or in it, so they took the chance and opened it. Then the news comes on that a wife just shot her husband. They go through many tests and try to investigate what's going on. Then the man comes to them again saying that their pre-teen son is blind and deaf, locked in the bathroom. He tells them they have a choice, either shoot the father (her husband) or allow the child to stay deaf

Notes:

How long will God allow evil to go on? He asks the same of us in our own lives. How long until you will live wholly for me? When will you be the light in this dark world? It's until we make a difference.

The Lord is not slow in keeping his promise, as some understand slowness. He is patient with you, not wanting anyone to perish, but everyone to come to repentance. 10 But the day of the Lord will come like a thief. The heavens will disappear with a roar; the elements will be destroyed by fire, and the earth and everything in it will be laid bare. 11 Since everything will be destroyed in this way, what kind of people ought you to be? You ought to live holy and godly lives - 2 Peter 3:9-11 NIV

In the same way, let your light shine before men, that they may see your good deeds and praise your Father in heaven. - Matthew 5:16 NIV

Greater love has no one than this, that someone lay down his life for his friends. - John 15:13 ESV

And he said to all, "If anyone would come after me, let him deny himself and take up his cross daily and follow me.24 For whoever would save his life will lose it, but whoever loses his life for my sake will save it. 25 For what does it profit a man if he gains the whole world and loses or forfeits himself? - Luke 9:23-25 ESV

We are afflicted in every way, but not crushed; perplexed, but not driven to despair; 9 persecuted, but not forsaken; struck down, but not destroyed; 10 always carrying in the body the death of Jesus, so that the life of Jesus may also be manifested in our bodies. 11 For we who live are always being given over to death for Jesus' sake, so that the life of Jesus also may be manifested in our mortal flesh. - 2 Corinthians 4:8-11 ESV

and blind, never hearing his parents' voices or seeing their faces. The parents eventually determine it would be better for him to live without a father than to live without his senses. Someone somewhere opened a box, and the woman shot her husband. An assistant asks the man how long will he keep testing people, he replies, "Until someone chooses correctly."

It looks like the people in the movie chose to have a "better" quality of life, rather than valuing life itself. You may wonder why does God allow these things to happen, how long? And he says until someone chooses life. We want to allow teenagers to have abortions so that they can have a better quality of life and the unborn child will not have to go through heartache.However, we don't chose to help them in their problems and love them and support them. We desire money and new cars and our possessions protected rather than risk giving a homeless man a twenty dollar bill, or heaven forbid invite him into our homes. We fear. We fear for our safety, and for the safety of our "quality of life". Jesus asks what would it matter if someone gained the whole world yet forfeited his soul. Jesus says no greater love could a man have than to lay down his life for his friends. He says if anyone were to come after him, he must deny himself, take up his cross and follow him. For whoever wants to save his life will lose it, but those who lose their life for his sake will find it.

When we recognize the One who is in control of it all has perfect love and limitless power and provision and wants us to join Him, inherit from Him all that He has, we must remember his purpose first and foremost is love. Everything has a purpose and everything is selfless. When we realize He is the one in whom we have security and safety we should be free to love.

At times I would get my hope up, many times actually, daily they would come crashing down. I didn't want to open anymore. It felt like someone punching me in the face and me just keeping my hands down. Eventually you can't take it, you are nearly destroyed and pass out. But Jesus did it. He somehow endured being flogged, beaten, beard pulled out, lashes, crucifixion, he endured it all for the love of the people that destroyed him. We aren't destroyed though. Neither

Notes:

As a prisoner for the Lord, then, I urge you to live a life worthy of the calling you have received. 2 Be completely humble and gentle; be patient, bearing with one another in love. 3 Make every effort to keep the unity of the Spirit through the bond of peace. 4 There is one body and one Spirit-- just as you were called to one hope when you were called-- 5 one Lord, one faith, one baptism; 6 one God and Father of all, who is over all and through all and in all. - Ephesians 4:1-6 NIV

was he, he rose again. God gave him life and gives us life as well.

God wants me to love. He wants me to love my wife as well as he has enabled me. That we would be humble and unified with one another, self-sacrificing, and encouraging. It's hard, but God wants love and character more than power. The power will be revealed, there will be healing, there will be evidence, but it must come with love. That's what God is looking for. For us to be broken, humble people that will love.

Notes:

And when Peter saw it he addressed the people: "Men of Israel, why do you wonder at this, or why do you stare at us, as though by our own power or piety we have made him walk? 13 The God of Abraham, the God of Isaac, and the God of Jacob, the God of our fathers, glorified his servant Jesus, whom you delivered over and denied in the presence of Pilate, when he had decided to release him. 16 And his name--by faith in his name--has made this man strong whom you see and know, and the faith that is through Jesus has given the man this perfect health in the presence of you all.
    - Acts 3:12-16 ESV

And now, Lord, look upon their threats and grant to your servants to continue to speak your word with all boldness, 30 while you stretch out your hand to heal, and signs and wonders are performed through the name of your holy servant Jesus." 31 And when they had prayed, the place in which they were gathered together was shaken, and they were all filled with the Holy Spirit and continued to speak the word of God with boldness.
    - Acts 4:29-31 ESV

And this is the confidence that we have toward him, that if we ask anything according to his will he hears us. 15 And if we know that he hears us in whatever we ask, we know that we have the requests that we have asked of him. - 1 John 5:14-15 ESV

So Jesus said to them, "Truly, truly, I say to you, the Son can do nothing of his own accord, but only what he sees the Father doing. For whatever the Father does, that the Son does likewise. - John 5:19 ESV

pray without ceasing, - 1 Thessalonians 5:17 ESV

In reading Acts we find that men were led by visions, or angels, or hearing the physical voice of God or impressions, but they all had clear direction. Philip was told to go down a desert road to minister to the Ethiopian eunuch (Acts 8:26). Ananias was told to go to Paul and heal his eyesight (Acts 9:12).

CHAPTER 7

OF ONE HEART

God's desire is for us to be in unity with him. Many think that we just need to try harder to exorcise that demon or receive a healing. We don't need to try harder to do anything. We need to seek God to allow Him to do what He said He would.

Look at Peter when he and John healed the lame man. "It was not by our piety or anything out of our own strength. We had nothing to do with the miracle. It was through faith in Jesus' name and that faith given us by God that this man stands whole." We never do anything. They prayed that God would do work through the hand of his servant Jesus, not them. It has nothing to do with us, absolutely nothing. People don't want to admit to that, and that's why some people are healed and some aren't. The belief is nothing, you can believe all you want for something to happen.

The Bible says the confidence we have is if we ask anything according to God's will, and Jesus said the stipulation to receiving was if we abided in Him and his Word in us. It's completely about humility and unity. He said even he himself did nothing of his own accord. God directed his actions. Does this mean you have to feel something before you heal, or be "led" to do a work? That's kind of the wrong question. We shouldn't switch God on and off and say, "I need to turn my spirituality on for a sec." No, we are supposed to pray without ceasing. We are supposed to live by the Spirit and in the

Notes:

And he went throughout all Galilee, teaching in their synagogues and proclaiming the gospel of the kingdom and healing every disease and every affliction among the people. - Matthew 4:23 ESV

A man with leprosy came and knelt before him and said, "Lord, if you are willing, you can make me clean." 3 Jesus reached out his hand and touched the man. "I am willing," he said. "Be clean!" Immediately he was cured of his leprosy. - Matthew 8:2-3 NIV

Some men brought to him a paralytic, lying on a mat. When Jesus saw their faith, he said to the paralytic, "Take heart, son; your sins are forgiven." 3 At this, some of the teachers of the law said to themselves, "This fellow is blaspheming!" 4 Knowing their thoughts, Jesus said, "Why do you entertain evil thoughts in your hearts? 5 Which is easier: to say, 'Your sins are forgiven,' or to say, 'Get up and walk'? 6 But so that you may know that the Son of Man has authority on earth to forgive sins . . ." Then he said to the paralytic, "Get up, take your mat and go home." 7 And the man got up and went home. - Matthew 9:2-7 NIV

Each of you should look not only to your own interests, but also to the interests of others. - Philippians 2:4 NIV

Greater love has no one than this, that he lay down his life for his friends.
   - John 15:13 NIV

By this all men will know that you are my disciples, if you love one another." - John 13:35 NIV

Do not be anxious about anything, but in everything, by prayer and petition, with thanksgiving, present your requests to God.
   - Philippians 4:6 NIV

Spirit. You need to know before you do something. You cannot boast in yourself or have confidence in yourself. You realize your own shortcomings and pursue intimacy with God, so you shouldn't have to ask that question. He would tell you why that person isn't healed and whether or not you would be wasting your breath. It's not a feeling, it's listening and obeying.

Yes God wants everyone healed, we know that is his will. What we don't know is how to go about it. Someone may need to be taught something first. They may need trust and belief and know whether or not God is willing. Case in point, the man with leprosy, he said "Lord if you are willing," and Jesus assured him saying, "I am willing, be clean." A lame man was brought to Jesus and he said to him said "Take heart, your sins are forgiven." Was there a reason he said that first? I'm sure. If anyone ever lived on purpose it was Jesus. I would assume since it was a common belief at the time, that sickness was thought to be God's punishment for sin, Jesus told the man he did not condemn him nor hold his sins against him, that is why he said "Take heart". Jesus constantly taught wherever he went explaining the heart of God. He told them not to worry about anything, not to do anything out of pride, just love.

There is unity in love. If you love someone you cause their desires to be your desires. The Bible says not to only care for your own interests but also the interests of others. No greater love can a man have than this to lay down his life for his friends. To sacrifice and counteract your instinctual desire for self-preservation for another person. Jesus said the world would recognize we belong to him by the way we love one another. The early church shared everything in common.

IF you delight yourself in the Lord, He will grant you the desires of your heart. Love should be mutual. As many would say in marriage, you give your spouse a 100% not 50/50. We do not grumble or complain because it is our desire to please God. When we pray we do not act out of anxiety because we know God knows our needs and desires to grant us our needs and wants, so we offer prayer in thanksgiving. God always loves us regardless of our actions, but

Notes:

If I have the gift of prophecy and can fathom all mysteries and all knowledge, and if I have a faith that can move mountains, but have not love, I am nothing. 3 If I give all I possess to the poor and surrender my body to the flames, but have not love, I gain nothing. 7 It always protects, always trusts, always hopes, always perseveres. 8 Love never fails.
    - 1 Corinthians 13:2-8 NIV

But the LORD came down to see the city and the tower that the men were building. 6 The LORD said, "If as one people speaking the same language they have begun to do this, then nothing they plan to do will be impossible for them. - Genesis 11:5-6 NIV

For them I sanctify myself, that they too may be truly sanctified. 20 "My prayer is not for them alone. I pray also for those who will believe in me through their message, 21 that all of them may be one, Father, just as you are in me and I am in you. May they also be in us so that the world may believe that you have sent me. 22 I have given them the glory that you gave me, that they may be one as we are one: 23 I in them and you in me. May they be brought to complete unity to let the world know that you sent me and have loved them even as you have loved me. 24 "Father, I want those you have given me to be with me where I am, and to see my glory, the glory you have given me because you loved me before the creation of the world. 25 "Righteous Father, though the world does not know you, I know you, and they know that you have sent me. 26 I have made you known to them, and will continue to make you known in order that the love you have for me may be in them and that I myself may be in them."
    - John 17:19-26 NIV

when we love it reciprocates and propels. It's difficult for me to find the right words, but being in unity with God brings power for miracles that we seek, and when we love others it keeps going on and gets stronger.

I realized what 1 Corinthians 13 meant when Paul said if I do works without love it profits me nothing. Unless I'm doing a work and joining myself and coming into unity with another person it does not come back to me. Not to say I get something out of it for myself, but when I cause someone else's desires to be mine I rejoice when they receive. I see our purpose has been fulfilled. This is why love doesn't envy. I see love as a circuit.

The tower of Babel had a perverted sense of unity, in that it was all for pride and not love. But there still was a since of unity, and when a house is united there is nothing to stand in the way. It's purpose can come about. God said nothing would stop those who are united. Also once again referring to 1 Corinthians 13, where love exists with unity, love never fails. There's nothing to stop it. It originates from God, flows through you, and out to another person.

Hopefully this makes some sense. The best object lesson I can use is being open to God and allowing him to flow through you like a metal object hitting a power line. Whoever you touch when connected to God is going to change. But if you do not reciprocate the love it would be like a branch hitting a power line, it has no power of its own and none flowing through it.

Jesus' prayer in John 17 was that we would be in him, him in us, us in the father, and everything unified. If ever you wanted to find out God's heart look at Jesus' prayer. His desire for love, unity, protection, and wholeness.

Notes:

As it is written, "Jacob I have loved, but Esau I have hated."
  - Romans 9:13 NKJV

Pursue peace with all people, and holiness, without which no one will see the Lord: 15 looking carefully lest anyone fall short of the grace of God; lest any root of bitterness springing up cause trouble, and by this many become defiled; 16 lest there be any fornicator or profane person like Esau, who for one morsel of food sold his birthright. 17 For you know that afterward, when he wanted to inherit the blessing, he was rejected, for he found no place for repentance, though he sought it diligently with tears.
  - Hebrews 12:14-17 NKJV

Profane means to make worthless. You hear a person add a little profanity to their sentence, those words mean nothing and make absolutely no sense, they are just fillers that kill the respect you would have for the person.

So the master commended the unjust steward because he had dealt shrewdly. For the sons of this world are more shrewd in their generation than the sons of light. 9 And I say to you, make friends for yourselves by unrighteous mammon, that when you fail, they may receive you into an everlasting home. 10 He who is faithful in what is least is faithful also in much; and he who is unjust in what is least is unjust also in much. 11 Therefore if you have not been faithful in the unrighteous mammon, who will commit to your trust the true riches? - Luke 16:8-11 NKJV

CHAPTER 8

HEART'S INTENT

"Jacob I loved, Esau I hated". That's an odd concept. First, why would God hate anyone, and second, why did he love the guy who cheated his brother out of his inheritance?

Esau was stupid! Look, his father was the promised son of Abraham. If you were to receive an inheritance from him you would become a nation recognized and favored by God. This isn't just a trust fund, this goes way beyond money and property. This was a bargain for God's favor and Esau sold it all for a bowl of stew. Jacob, as deceitful as he was, recognized the value that was in his father's inheritance. He treated it with utmost respect. So the difference between the two brothers? One of them actually cared. Cared enough to craft a plan to receive it for himself. Esau basically profaned the promise of God. What more can you do to evoke his wrath? That's why he said "Esau I hated."

Jesus tells a parable about a man who didn't keep his accounts with his master. He wrote down a fraction of what everyone owed his master so that they would take care of him when he was fired. He put thought into what he was doing. Jesus is not saying sin is OK, but the sinful people seem to put more thought into what they do than the self-righteous. He basically says, if you cannot recognize value in the small things, if you cannot put thought into how to spend money, how can you be trusted with things that are more

Notes:

"Be careful not to do your 'acts of righteousness' before men, to be seen by them. If you do, you will have no reward from your Father in heaven.
    - Matthew 6:1 NIV

But I tell you that men will have to give account on the day of judgment for every careless word they have spoken. 37 For by your words you will be acquitted, and by your words you will be condemned."
    - Matthew 12:36-37 NIV

The tongue also is a fire, a world of evil among the parts of the body. It corrupts the whole person, sets the whole course of his life on fire, and is itself set on fire by hell. - James 3:6 NIV

The tongue has the power of life and death, and those who love it will eat its fruit. - Proverbs 18:21 NIV

Just as damaging as a mad man shooting a lethal weapon 19 is someone who lies to a friend and then says, "I was only joking."
    - Proverbs 26:18-19 NLT

So whether you eat or drink or whatever you do, do it all for the glory of God. - 1 Corinthians 10:31 NIV

And whatever you do, whether in word or deed, do it all in the name of the Lord Jesus, giving thanks to God the Father through him. - Colossians 3:17 NIV

Whatever you do, work at it with all your heart, as working for the Lord, not for men, - Colossians 3:23 NIV

important?

God desires us to actually think. The Pharisees did not take into account why the law was written, just that it was necessary and Jesus scolded them. They were so focused on looking good they didn't look for purpose. Jesus said, "Don't perform acts of righteousness before men to be seen by them." It's a temptation to keep us from being genuine. He doesn't mind if people see a good act, it doesn't mean don't show your devotion outside the home. It means whatever you do do it for God and not man. Jesus was looking out for the people saying, "If you want a reward, don't cheat yourself out of one trying to get men to notice you."

Also look at your day to day actions. What do we say? I had a little discussion with someone in high school and they didn't understand the big deal about profanity, because they were just words. I asked, "Are you a Christian?" "Yeah." "So do you know how the universe came into existence?" "God spoke." "Just words huh?" Then they understood. It's not that it's a bad word, it's that we use these words carelessly, or intentionally to provoke anger in someone. Jesus said that we would be held accountable for every careless word we have spoken. By our words we would be acquitted or condemned. James expounds on this idea saying that the tongue is an unruly evil. Proverbs says the power of life and death is in the tongue. Lying without thinking of the consequences: the boy who cried wolf, well proverbs sums that story up in a single verse: "As dangerous as a mad man shooting arrows is the man who lies and then says, 'I was only joking'."

How we work, how we dress, how we act it all says something about our character. If we represent Christ and are to show his love to others so that they will desire and come to know him, we have to display his character. Do we dress modestly or appropriately? Does it look like we care? Do we do work to the best of our ability no matter how small the task? It's not the task God is concerned about, it's the character you have and how you show him you care, whether cleaning toilets or managing a business.

Notes:

"Do not give dogs what is sacred; do not throw your pearls to pigs. If you do, they may trample them under their feet, and then turn and tear you to pieces. - Matthew 7:6 NIV

Jesus does say to give to the one who asks, but also says the above. Discern a person's heart and what they will do with it. That does not mean assuming a homeless man he will be alcohol or drugs. Knowing what to give and who to give it to. Will the gift of money, time, effort be appreciated and used? Looking at Acts Chapter 4 the crippled man was asking for alms, but Peter and John gave him what he truly needed in healing him. First and foremost we need to know how to listen to God and then act accordingly benefitting others.

"Come to me, all you who are weary and burdened, and I will give you rest.
    - Matthew 11:28 NIV

Cast your cares on the LORD and he will sustain you; he will never let the righteous fall. - Psalm 55:22 NIV

Cast all your anxiety on him because he cares for you. - 1 Peter 5:7 NIV

Let us not become weary in doing good, for at the proper time we will reap a harvest if we do not give up. 10 Therefore, as we have opportunity, let us do good to all people, especially to those who belong to the family of believers. - Galatians 6:9-10 NIV

Solomon had the position of king and was humble enough to ask God, "How can I rule a nation that bears your name? Please give me wisdom!" There are responsibilities we know God requires of us and we need to operate in wisdom. Not just throw money everywhere, not say yes to every person, but have discernment asking "God what do you desire of me personally, you who care about the details, where should this money go, where should I be directed." Jesus says "Do not give to dogs what is sacred or cast your pearls to pigs. Or else they will trample them under their feet and then turn and tear you to pieces."

It's difficult to maintain this mentality, because when we get frustrated we typically throw our hands in the air and say "I don't care anymore." We can't handle everything thrown at us, we don't have infinite patience, but Jesus says come and you'll find rest. Cast your cares upon the Lord for he cares for you. We get hurt by a spouse, family or friend and just start throwing out words that we regret. Step back and remember, "Wait, God you know the intent of men's hearts, give me understanding." Don't grow weary in well doing, don't get frustrated, put your heart into whatever you do or say.

Notes:

For it is by grace you have been saved, through faith--and this not from yourselves, it is the gift of God-- Ephesians 2:8 NIV

By faith in the name of Jesus, this man whom you see and know was made strong. It is Jesus' name and the faith that comes through him that has given this complete healing to him, as you can all see. - Acts 3:16 NIV

Sometimes Jesus words are a little difficult to understand, so comparing the gospels is a good way to gain some clarity.

Jesus rebuked the demon, and it came out of the boy, and he was healed from that moment. 19 Then the disciples came to Jesus in private and asked, "Why couldn't we drive it out?" 20 He replied, "Because you have so little faith. I tell you the truth, if you have faith as small as a mustard seed, you can say to this mountain, 'Move from here to there' and it will move. Nothing will be impossible for you. " - Matthew 17:18-20 NIV

The apostles said to the LORD, "Increase our faith!" 6 He replied, "If you have faith as small as a mustard seed, you can say to this mulberry tree, 'Be uprooted and planted in the sea,' and it will obey you. - Luke 17:5-6 NIV

They were all terrified when they saw him. But Jesus spoke to them at once. "It's all right," he said. "I am here! Don't be afraid." 51 Then he climbed into the boat, and the wind stopped. They were astonished at what they saw. 52 They still didn't understand the significance of the miracle of the multiplied loaves, for their hearts were hard and they did not believe.
   - Mark 6:50-52 NLT

The disciples had forgotten to bring bread, except for one loaf they had with them in the boat. 15 "Be careful," Jesus warned them. "Watch out for the yeast of the Pharisees and that of Herod." 16 They discussed this with one another and said, "It is because we have no bread." 17 Aware of their discussion, Jesus asked them: "Why are you talking about having no bread? Do you still not see or understand? Are your hearts hardened? 18 Do you have eyes but fail to see, and ears but fail to hear? And don't you remember? 19 When I broke the five loaves for the five thousand, how many basketfuls of pieces did you pick up?" "Twelve," they replied. 20 "And when I broke the seven loaves for the four thousand, how many basketfuls of pieces did you pick up?" They answered, "Seven." 21 He said to them, "Do you still not understand?" - Mark 8:14-21 NIV

CHAPTER 9

LOVE ALWAYS TRUSTS

Trust is everything. People think they need to build their faith before they can trust God. You can't build trust. Either you have it or you don't. You think your faith does the work, but you don't have faith without God. That faith is a gift, not a work. God does the work by his grace. Since God is all powerful you don't need to build your faith to do a grand work, because God does the work and he doesn't need the exercise.

Think of it this way. It is difficult to believe to move a mountain because you think by your own effort in mustering up faith it's up to you, but you forget that your prayer requires great faith. You do more than move mountains, you move the creator of the mountains. Which is more difficult to believe: that you matter to God, or that you can move a microscopic mountain compared to Almighty God? This is why Jesus said, if you have faith the size of a mustard seed you can say to this mountain move from here to there. We keep thinking the disciples didn't have enough faith, but Jesus said that the mustard seed was the smallest of all seeds. It isn't that they lacked faith; they lacked faithfulness. They saw miracles and even performed miracles, but they rarely ever yielded their hearts to God. They often focused on their own effort, which is why they couldn't drive out the demon. They do the same thing we do. "It worked last time, but what about this time?" This is why when Jesus talked about "yeast of the Pharisees and Sadducees" they worried about bringing bread.

Notes:

Aware of their discussion, Jesus asked, "You of little faith, why are you talking among yourselves about having no bread? - Matthew 16:8 NIV

But Jesus immediately said to them: "Take courage! It is I. Don't be afraid." 28 "Lord, if it's you," Peter replied, "tell me to come to you on the water." 29 "Come," he said. Then Peter got down out of the boat, walked on the water and came toward Jesus. 30 But when he saw the wind, he was afraid and, beginning to sink, cried out, "Lord, save me!" 31 Immediately Jesus reached out his hand and caught him. "You of little faith," he said, "why did you doubt?" 32 And when they climbed into the boat, the wind died down. 33 Then those who were in the boat worshiped him, saying, "Truly you are the Son of God." - Matthew 14:27-33 NIV

And when he comes, he will convince the world of its sin, and of God's righteousness, and of the coming judgment. 9 The world's sin is unbelief in me. - John 16:8-9 NLT

You want something but don't get it. You kill and covet, but you cannot have what you want. You quarrel and fight. You do not have, because you do not ask God... 8 Come near to God and he will come near to you. Wash your hands, you sinners, and purify your hearts, you double-minded.
    - James 4:2, 8 NIV

For the Scriptures tell us, "Abraham believed God, so God declared him to be righteous." - Romans 4:3 NLT

When Adam sinned, sin entered the entire human race. Adam's sin brought death, so death spread to everyone, for everyone sinned.
    - Romans 5:12 NLT

But when he asks, he must believe and not doubt, because he who doubts is like a wave of the sea, blown and tossed by the wind. 7 That man should not think he will receive anything from the Lord; 8 he is a double-minded man, unstable in all he does. - James 1:6-8 NIV

They already saw the bread multiplied for thousands. That is why Jesus said they had little faith, their hearts were hard. We have to look at everything in context.

We get so tied up with the problems and the lies of Satan that we forget who God is, how big he is, how good he is. We talk to him without looking to him. If we would just behold him then we could believe. Peter walked on the water as long as his focus was on Jesus, and as soon as he glanced at the waves, he sank. You have to look to God for the solution. This is why we worship. We sing about the character of God so that we can readjust our focus. Stop focusing on what you can't do, and start focusing on what God can do.

Trust is not just believing for a prayer request either. Jesus says the world's sin is unbelief in him. That's pretty literal. When we don't trust that he'll meet our needs, we steal. When we don't trust he will defend us, we kill. When we don't trust all things work out, we lie. When we don't trust he'll give us our desires, we covet. The list goes on. Abraham believed and it was credited to him as righteousness. Adam doubted and the whole world fell apart.

Many times we aren't honest with ourselves and we will say God is good, but doubt his character. We ask why there isn't healing, why there isn't provision, and why did our marriage go south? We build up animosity, but try to tuck it away and refuse to acknowledge it. We become two-faced. God can't work like that. I mentioned it when talking about a broken heart.

We have fears because we lack understanding, how do you trust something you don't know? It's impossible. You have skepticism from the get-go. Teachers and preachers are no help. They say "I don't want a God I can understand, because then he wouldn't be God and I wouldn't need him." One of the dumbest things I ever heard. If I understand everything, I understand my need for God and that there is no hope outside of him. Once I understand him we can trust one another and actually do his work. God does not want to be mysterious.

Notes:

He who did not spare his own Son, but gave him up for us all--how will he not also, along with him, graciously give us all things? - Romans 8:32 NIV

This is how God showed his love among us: He sent his one and only Son into the world that we might live through him. - 1 John 4:9 NIV

"As for the person who hears my words but does not keep them, I do not judge him. For I did not come to judge the world, but to save it.
    - John 12:47 NIV

For I know the plans I have for you," declares the LORD, "plans to prosper you and not to harm you, plans to give you hope and a future. 12 Then you will call upon me and come and pray to me, and I will listen to you. 13 You will seek me and find me when you seek me with all your heart.
    - Jeremiah 29:11-13 NIV

If any of you lacks wisdom, he should ask God, who gives generously to all without finding fault, and it will be given to him. - James 1:5 NIV

And we know that in all things God works for the good of those who love him, who have been called according to his purpose. - Romans 8:28 NIV

The Lord is not slack concerning His promise, as some count slackness, but is longsuffering toward us, not willing that any should perish but that all should come to repentance. - 2 Peter 3:9 NKJV

Because narrow is the gate and difficult is the way which leads to life, and there are few who find it. - Matthew 7:14 NKJV

Jesus speaks of being a rock of offense, anyone who stumbles over it will be broken, him on whom it falls will be ground to powder (Matthew 21:44). Meaning if you accept him you will be humbled, if you reject and are prideful, you will be destroyed.

Two of the biggest reasons we do not trust God for something is one: we don't think we deserve it, or two: we are afraid of the catch or consequences. There shouldn't be any fear as to whether or not God is willing to heal a child on his deathbed. "God showed his love in this, that while we were yet sinners Christ died for us... If he did not even spare his own Son, but gave him up as a sacrifice for us, will he not much more gives all things?" God does not condemn, Jesus said that on the earth. "I came not to judge the world, but to save it. " God is merciful. Another scripture many of us love quoting Jeremiah 29:11, saying "I know the plans I have for you. Plans for good not for destruction. To give you a future and a hope." Why should we be afraid that God is going to punish us for asking for a gift? God is not out to get us, and he hates us thinking we have to earn anything from him. James says that God gives freely to everyone without finding fault. Freely. There's no catch with God. You may be surprised at how he operates, but everything works out for our good.

In Romans 9:14-24, Paul speaks of why men reject God and that God can harden hearts. The question is why would God create a man he knows is going to refuse him? God knew that whatever he did would harden Pharaoh's heart rather than break it. This gave God the opportunity to send plagues to make surrounding nations fear the God of Israel. He used a person he knew would refuse his will to still bring something good, he didn't waste a person. God would get glory regardless of how he acted.

Since we don't understand him we assume that anything that happens, whether good or bad is his will. But if God says that he isn't willing that any should perish, and then says very few actually make it to heaven, then obviously not everything that happens is his will. How can that be? Our free will. There's a law that God operates by and it's called holiness. God does not operate in a lie, he does not deal with corruption, he doesn't accept those things. We can either choose to join Satan or choose to join Christ. I know Calvinists are scratching their heads and saying, "but God is Sovereign." I completely agree that God is sovereign. How else could God use so many screw-ups for his glory? The sovereignty of

Notes:

Many are the plans in a man's heart, but it is the LORD's purpose that prevails. - Proverbs 19:21 NIV

Satan goes to God to ask permission to inflict Job (Job 1:12). God also sees Israel stumbling and allows the devil to tempt Adam to bring judgment on Israel (1 Chronicles 21:1. 2 Samuel 24:1). An evil king God causes to die as a result of his own pride by allowing a lying spirit to enter prophets (1 Kings 22:22). However, the one man that stays true to God prophesies the truth. This shows that God gave that king a choice with full knowledge of what was to happen.

God means that He knows everything that has ever happened and will happen, that everything that does happen he uses for some sort of good, and that no matter what happens his purpose always prevails. Satan can do nothing without God's permission, and God allows things to happen to bring us to a place where we can't sit on the fence anymore; we have to choose.

Notes:

In the beginning was the Word, and the Word was with God, and the Word was God. - John 1:1 NIV

Moses said to God, "Suppose I go to the Israelites and say to them, 'The God of your fathers has sent me to you,' and they ask me, 'What is his name?' Then what shall I tell them?" 14 God said to Moses, "I AM WHO I AM. This is what you are to say to the Israelites: 'I AM has sent me to you.' " - Genesis 3:13-14 NIV

This is the book of the generations of Adam. When God created man, he made him in the likeness of God - Genesis 5:1 ESV

You are of your father the devil, and your will is to do your father's desires. He was a murderer from the beginning, and has nothing to do with the truth, because there is no truth in him. When he lies, he speaks out of his own character, for he is a liar and the father of lies. - John 8:44 ESV

and to put on the new self, created after the likeness of God in true righteousness and holiness. - Ephesians 4:24 ESV

for "'In him we live and move and have our being; as even some of your own poets have said, "'For we are indeed his offspring.' - Acts 17:28 ESV

The thief comes only to steal and kill and destroy; I have come that they may have life, and have it to the full. - John 10:10 NIV

For the wrath of God is revealed from heaven against all ungodliness and unrighteousness of men, who by their unrighteousness suppress the truth. 19 For what can be known about God is plain to them, because God has shown it to them. 20 For his invisible attributes, namely, his eternal power and divine nature, have been clearly perceived, ever since the creation of the world, in the things that have been made. So they are without excuse. 21 For although they knew God, they did not honor him as God or give thanks to him, but they became futile in their thinking, and their foolish hearts were darkened. 22 Claiming to be wise, they became fools, 23 and exchanged the glory of the immortal God for images resembling mortal man and birds and animals and creeping things. 24 Therefore God gave them up in the lusts of their hearts to impurity, to the dishonoring of their bodies among themselves, 25 because they exchanged the truth about God for a lie and worshiped and served the creature rather than the Creator, who is blessed forever! Amen. - Romans 1:18-25 ESV

CHAPTER 10

TRUTH

I am the way, the truth, and the life. -John 14:6 NIV

One of the most audacious and most profound things Jesus said. This is not just a religious statement. This small, straightforward statement explains everything.

In the beginning God spoke a word. In the beginning was the Word. Without God nothing was made. God in short made everything by his word. His name is "I am". All existence, all life came from him. Whatever he speaks is. He is not capable of speaking a lie. Whatever he speaks happens. He is the way everything works, exists, lives. He is the way, the truth, the life. Satan lies. He is completely anti-God. He steals, kills, and destroys. So when God creates man in his image and all the sudden he follows Satan, the entire world is shaken. The world was created by truth and destroyed by a lie. This is why sin is such a big issue. We destroy the work of God by joining Satan in believing his lies.

When you think about it knowing all this, lies and sin take on a whole new perspective. I'm destroying the work of God when I sin. He made everything good and perfect and I more than tarnished it. I gave it no value, no consideration, I trampled it. I need a savior, I need someone to make this right.

Notes:

The good man brings good things out of the good stored up in his heart, and the evil man brings evil things out of the evil stored up in his heart. For out of the overflow of his heart his mouth speaks. - Luke 6:45 NIV

May the words of my mouth and the meditation of my heart be pleasing in your sight, O LORD, my Rock and my Redeemer. - Psalm 19:14 NIV

Some Jews who went around driving out evil spirits tried to invoke the name of the Lord Jesus over those who were demon-possessed. They would say, "In the name of Jesus, whom Paul preaches, I command you to come out." 14 Seven sons of Sceva, a Jewish chief priest, were doing this. 15 [One day] the evil spirit answered them, "Jesus I know, and I know about Paul, but who are you?" 16 Then the man who had the evil spirit jumped on them and overpowered them all. He gave them such a beating that they ran out of the house naked and bleeding. 17 When this became known to the Jews and Greeks living in Ephesus, they were all seized with fear, and the name of the Lord Jesus was held in high honor. - Acts 19:13-17 NIV

For it is by believing in your heart that you are made right with God, and it is by confessing with your mouth that you are saved. - Romans 10:10 NLT

I have hidden your word in my heart that I might not sin against you.
    - Psalm 119:11 NIV

I know this is difficult to understand because it is so abstract, but there is a battle raging on earth. Paul talks about the flesh raging against the Spirit. We see the corruption of the world that came as a result of a lie and need to be reminded of the truth. God was pushed out when Adam rejected the truth, he wants us to invite him back in. Lying is such a big deal because it is denying God all over again. Jesus prays in John 17 that we would be sanctified by the truth, meaning given over completely to the truth and believing God entirely, that Jesus himself would dwell in our hearts and cause us to serve him whole heartedly. Jesus said that we should worship in Spirit and in truth, meaning he wants us united with him. Just listening and believing is worship to him, and then of course acting in love.

There are books out that speak of the power of words. I don't like focusing on having control. I want God to have control. I don't speak positive words to direct my future. Jesus said the words show what is in a man's heart. It's your heart that needs to be right. May the words of my mouth and the meditation of my heart be acceptable... -

If we speak words that are not from the heart they have no power. The seven sons of Sceva tried in vain using Jesus' name. Even the way to be saved is not just confessing with your mouth, but also believing with your heart. Hiding God's word in your heart changes your heart, changes your words, and then that is power. That is the power of God working in you.

You will know the truth and the truth will set you free.
- John 8:32

When you know Jesus and his heart there is no fear. He doesn't condemn. He wants to shed light on the issue so you can see and understand. God did not want Adam to eat from the tree of knowledge of good and evil because he didn't want Adam to know evil, or the absence of God. There is nothing outside of God. It was a temptation with an empty promise and it still is today. God doesn't want us without him. The decision is not "good or bad", "Jesus or another religion", it's "all or nothing". Otherwise it doesn't make sense why God would allow those guilty of sin into heaven, or why God would condemn someone to hell for believing another religion. There's really no choice. It's all or nothing. You cannot save a man with a lie. Say "I'm tossing you a line" to someone hanging off a cliff when there is no rope. Just because you said it and the guy believed it didn't make it true nor did it help the man. There is an absolute truth and Jesus is it.

Notes:

What do you think? If a man has a hundred sheep, and one of them has gone astray, does he not leave the ninety-nine on the mountains and go in search of the one that went astray? - Matthew 18:12 ESV

I tell you the truth, until heaven and earth disappear, not the smallest letter, not the least stroke of a pen, will by any means disappear from the Law until everything is accomplished. - Matthew 5:18 NIV

I tell you, he will see that they get justice, and quickly. However, when the Son of Man comes, will he find faith on the earth?" - Luke 18:8 NIV

In all my prayers for all of you, I always pray with joy 5 because of your partnership in the gospel from the first day until now, 6 being confident of this, that he who began a good work in you will carry it on to completion until the day of Christ Jesus. - Philippians 1:4-6 NIV

News about him spread all over Syria, and people brought to him all who were ill with various diseases, those suffering severe pain, the demon-possessed, those having seizures, and the paralyzed, and he healed them.
     - Matthew 4:24 NIV

Aware of this, Jesus withdrew from that place. Many followed him, and he healed all their sick, - Matthew 12:15 NIV

You made all the delicate, inner parts of my body and knit me together in my mother's womb. 14 Thank you for making me so wonderfully complex! Your workmanship is marvelous -- and how well I know it.
     - Psalm 139:13-14 NLT

This makes for harmony among the members, so that all the members care for each other equally. 26 If one part suffers, all the parts suffer with it, and if one part is honored, all the parts are glad. 27 Now all of you together are Christ's body, and each one of you is a separate and necessary part of it.
     - 1 Corinthians 12:25-27 NLT
This regards both the church and the human body.

CHAPTER 11

HOLY

It was said that the good shepherd left the 99 to search for the one. Why do that? So he could have all of the fold. He wants wholeness. He wants things complete, to think that he would accept anything less is to doubt his character. He doesn't leave things undone. Not the smallest letter or the least stroke of a pen would be done away with. He cares about details, and to think that he would wait forever... he desires to act quickly. So when I see sickness or ailment I start to get excited knowing I can see God operate in a way that isn't typical in this world. It's an exciting thing to see the authority and the gifts that he's given us.

Look at healing this way. Someone might believe for a cold to go away, but can't believe for something "bigger". If it is all up to God and us trusting his character, then it would be like someone drawing a mustache on the Mona Lisa and putting a little wart on her cheek. Is God going to say, "That wart is really bugging me" erase it and leave the mustache? Your body is a beautiful and complex work of art with billions of cells all working together. To say that he is more faithful to fix the little things is crazy. He's a perfectionist. He wants everything right regardless of the size.

The Bible says that He who began a good work in us will be faithful to complete it. He desires us to get out of the way. We often don't want to fix the problem, we distract ourselves with

Notes:

Jacob was reunited with Esau through God's grace, Joseph reunited with his brothers, Moses reunited with his brother Aaron, etc. God wants there to be love and not animosity towards others. He tries to make our heart right, often getting us into uncomfortable situations so that our hearts can heal from heart. He doesn't desire for families to be broken. He wants to make everything whole. Remember that Jesus said to first be reconciled to your brother before you present a gift at the altar (Matthew 5:24). He desires love more than anything, because he loves all of us.

But the fruit of the Spirit is love, joy, peace, patience, kindness, goodness, faithfulness, 23 gentleness and self-control. Against such things there is no law. - Galatians 5:22 -23 NIV

Be perfect, therefore, as your heavenly Father is perfect.
      - Matthew 5:48 NIV
This verse is prefaced by Jesus telling people to love everyone and show kindness, whether they are enemy or friend, showing no partiality. God is not petty, nor should we be.

entertainment to avoid the problem. We think that this is happiness. "If I get enough good to outweigh the bad, or not look at the bad, I'll be fine and happy." God is not interested in your happiness. He desires wholeness and with that wholeness comes joy. Something that isn't fleeting, because it's been completed.

God didn't rest the seventh day, until after he completed everything in the first six. He doesn't procrastinate, and he doesn't want us to lie around either. Sometimes he puts pain and suffering in our way to get us to come to him, to get us to realize we have some unfinished business: restoring relationships with friends and family, becoming a better husband, wife, father, mother, brother, or sister. It's mostly about relationships. We need sort of *a Christmas Carol* moment or *It's a Wonderful Life* moment, to see the importance of our life and how we affect those around us. There is no reason to think that one is a failure or worthless. We often have so much guilt for doing or not doing something that we shut the world out by entertainment, or even working too much.

We don't begin to grasp the concept of holiness: whole, perfect, good. Since we've never seen perfection we see holiness as just rules and regulations, something that will ultimately make us poor and destitute. Holiness is partaking in the very nature of God. It leads us to love, joy, peace goodness, faithfulness, kindness, understanding...perfection.

As I wrote earlier, the law only consisted of doing unto others as you would have them do to you. Holiness is abiding by that law through the love or through the Spirit that God gave us.

Notes:

None of them shall teach his neighbor, and none his brother, saying, 'Know the Lord,' for all shall know Me, from the least of them to the greatest of them. - Hebrews 8:11 NKJV

Heal the sick, raise the dead, cleanse those who have leprosy, drive out demons. Freely you have received, freely give. - Matthew 10:8 NIV

However, as it is written: "No eye has seen, no ear has heard, no mind has conceived what God has prepared for those who love him"-- 10 but God has revealed it to us by his Spirit. The Spirit searches all things, even the deep things of God - 1 Corinthians 2:9-10 NIV

This mystery is that through the gospel the Gentiles are heirs together with Israel, members together of one body, and sharers together in the promise in Christ Jesus. 7 I became a servant of this gospel by the gift of God's grace given me through the working of his power. 8 Although I am less than the least of all God's people, this grace was given me: to preach to the Gentiles the unsearchable riches of Christ, 9 and to make plain to everyone the administration of this mystery, which for ages past was kept hidden in God, who created all things. 10 His intent was that now, through the church, the manifold wisdom of God should be made known to the rulers and authorities in the heavenly realms, 11 according to his eternal purpose which he accomplished in Christ Jesus our Lord. 12 In him and through faith in him we may approach God with freedom and confidence.
    - Ephesians 3:6-12 NIV

Meaning, though Satan tried to destroy God's creation we prove to him that God is greater and wiser than he. Him redeeming us and us trusting him, yielding to him, allowing him to do a work in us, shows Satan he has no power, no authority over us any longer. That God would not just have Israel, but people of every nation. He would take all of us.

CHAPTER 12

HEART REVEALED

God wants us to get to a place where we understand and trust him. Where there is no more guesswork, but confidence and certainty. Not have to look for signs wondering if this is his will, or what did he say, what did he mean by what he said, and constantly worry. He wants our heart joined to his so that we will know him even better than we know ourselves. Because he is faithful. He doesn't have mood swings. He is certain.

Many don't want to have the responsibility, so they play as though God is mysterious. For instance, praying about a sick or severely injured person "if it be your will, let him live." What does Jesus say? The thief's purpose is to steal, kill, and destroy, but my purpose is to bring life and that more abundant. Yes it's God's will to heal, and God's will to restore life. The disciples, and us included, were told to heal the sick, raise the dead, cleanse those with leprosy, drive out demons. Jesus said "Freely you have received, freely give."

I believe this is why it was said "No eye has seen, no ear has heard, no mind has conceived what God has prepared for those who love him" because it is God himself in us. He was completely intangible. He was so holy if someone touch the ark of the covenant he dropped dead. But now he has made us holy so that we could be with him. This was his plan all along. For the people that were longing to be with him, he brought heaven down to them. And we get impatient for heaven, God even more so! Look at what he delivered! He couldn't withhold it any longer, he gave us a peek at

Notes:

14 For this reason I kneel before the Father, 15 from whom his whole family in heaven and on earth derives its name. 16 I pray that out of his glorious riches he may strengthen you with power through his Spirit in your inner being, 17 so that Christ may dwell in your hearts through faith. And I pray that you, being rooted and established in love, 18 may have power, together with all the saints, to grasp how wide and long and high and deep is the love of Christ, 19 and to know this love that surpasses knowledge-- that you may be filled to the measure of all the fullness of God. 20 Now to him who is able to do immeasurably more than all we ask or imagine, according to his power that is at work within us, 21 to him be glory in the church and in Christ Jesus throughout all generations, for ever and ever! Amen. - Ephesians 3:14-21

"The kingdom of heaven is like a king who prepared a wedding banquet for his son. 3 He sent his servants to those who had been invited to the banquet to tell them to come, but they refused to come. 4 "Then he sent some more servants and said, 'Tell those who have been invited that I have prepared my dinner: My oxen and fattened cattle have been butchered, and everything is ready. Come to the wedding banquet.' 5 "But they paid no attention and went off--one to his field, another to his business. 6 The rest seized his servants, mistreated them and killed them. 7 The king was enraged. He sent his army and destroyed those murderers and burned their city. 8 "Then he said to his servants, 'The wedding banquet is ready, but those I invited did not deserve to come. 9 Go to the street corners and invite to the banquet anyone you find.' 10 So the servants went out into the streets and gathered all the people they could find, both good and bad, and the wedding hall was filled with guests. 11 "But when the king came in to see the guests, he noticed a man there who was not wearing wedding clothes. 12 'Friend,' he asked, 'how did you get in here without wedding clothes?' The man was speechless. 13 "Then the king told the attendants, 'Tie him hand and foot, and throw him outside, into the darkness, where there will be weeping and gnashing of teeth.' 14 "For many are invited, but few are chosen." - Matthew 22:2-14 NIV

From what I have read, wedding clothes were provided by the king at this sort of banquet. Meaning God offered his righteousness to everyone, but this man refused to accept the gift to put on this new nature. He did not act in holiness. So God was enraged at this man who refused the gift. It's like wanting to go to heaven, but not wanting a thing to do with God. Because as I said, holiness is taking part in his nature which we are able to do. He enables us to love. That's what it boils down to.

Christmas; men were able to see the face of God. When Pentecost came we became able to see the heart of God.

For those looking for revival this is it. Recognizing the Holy Spirit and not stifling him. Listening intently, desiring to be consumed by God and his holy nature. We don't need to question whether we are good enough, or wonder how many works we have to do to prove we are serious. It's all about heart. The Pharisees tried showing "devotion". We can finally say with certainty, "This is God's will and I am confidently joining him. He desires to use me even if I am the least of everyone, or the worst 'screw-up'. There is no doubting him, nor the work that he started in me." You should see how much he loves you and be able to share that love with others.

This is an invitation. Jesus compared the Kingdom of Heaven to a wedding banquet. God has finally made a way for us to be married into his family through his son. It represents redemption and he wants everyone to partake in it. Many are not interested but are more concerned with their own business, making money, gaining prestige, focusing on them and their work. So he invites those that have nothing, the rejects, those who feel honored to be invited to a banquet and not burdened or obligated to go.

There is "nothing" to lose.

Will you accept the invitation?

ABOUT THE AUTHOR

Basically I'm just an average person with some cool ideas. Nothing really praise-worthy. No degree, no accolades. I have a wife and kids. (We had another son since this book came out.)

I try to keep a blog. Sometimes I don't write in it as much because I'm focusing on writing another book, but there are a number of good articles at www.rbbamburg.com And then in addition to that I have a ministry YouTube channel RBBamburg and a personal one called VloggerTroubles if you're curious what my life is like. Forewarning though, just about everything I do is sporadic.

ALSO AVAILABLE FROM
R.B.BAMBURG

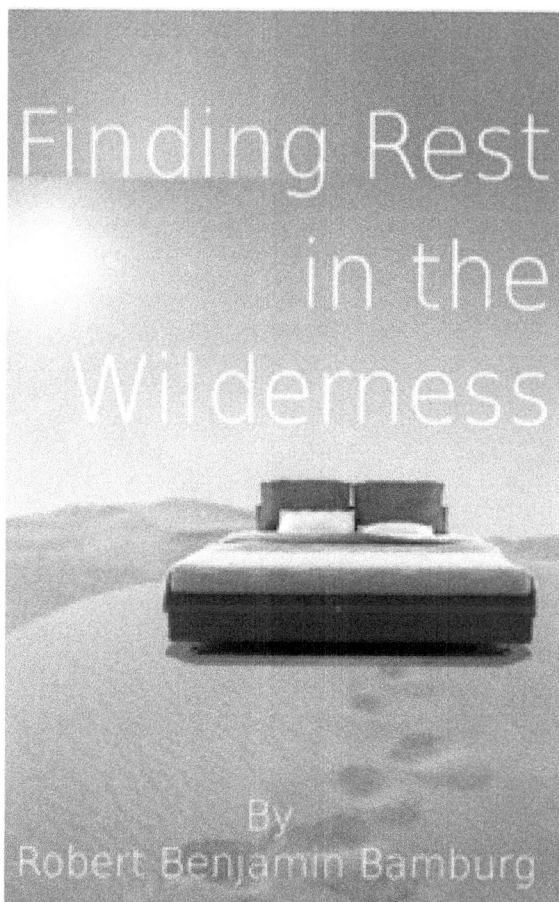

God promised the Israelites a land flowing with milk and honey, and expected them to somehow relax while traveling through the barren desert. But during that time, He dropped food out of the sky, spewed water from rocks, made sure their clothes didn't wear out, and gave them direction by pillars of cloud and fire. We also somehow miss his interventions like they did while we are waiting for heaven. Finding Rest in the Wilderness helps you see where God is when everything looks wrong, and you can't seem to feel him. He isn't playing hard to get, in fact, He's trying harder than ever to show himself

www.ingramcontent.com/pod-product-compliance
Lightning Source LLC
Chambersburg PA
CBHW072208090426
42740CB00012B/2442